Raising a
Spiritual
Child

A Jewish Perspective

Stephanie Hubert Schneider, Ph.D.

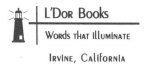

L'Dor Books
Words that illuminate

Irvine, California

For information on this book:

L'Dor Books
5319 University Drive # 305
Irvine, CA 92612
ldorbooks@usa.net

ISBN 0-9679164-3-7
Library of Congress Card Number 00-19031

5   4   3   2   1

Contents

Introduction 1

1 "*What's a Parent to Do?*" 7

Putting God in the Picture 7
A Call to the Heart 9
Yes, We Can! 11

2 *The Four Factors of Faith* 15

Discovering the Faith Factors 15
Facts—The Search for Understanding 17
Feeling—the Search for Comfort 18
Friends—The Search for Relationship 18
Focus—the Search for Guidance 19
The Balance of "Four" 20
Which Aspect for Whom? 21

3 *Watching our Children Grow* 27

Of Piaget and Erikson 28
The Religious World of Preschoolers 30
Spirituality in Elementary School 32
God in the Middle School Years 34
Faith in the Teen Years 36
How To Parent A Teen 38

4 *Profiling Your Child's Faith* 41

Profiling your Child 43
Activities 44
Personality 46
Environment & Family 48
How To Use The Benefit Profiler 51
Children's Benefits Profile 51

5 *Different Paths, Different Choices* 55

"Just the Facts, Ma'am": The Path of Intellect 56
Once more with Feeling: The Path of Emotion 60
When Friendship Counts Most:Relationship 62
Focus on Focus: The Factor of Guidance 65

6 *Teaching Values, Teaching Torah* 69

Using the Aspects in Teaching Values 72
Values guiding behavior towards others 75
Values Guiding our Personal Behavior 79

7 *Talking About God* 85

The Four Factors and God 87
"What is God like?" 89
"Why do We Pray?" 90
"What does God want from us?" 92
"What is sin, and why is there evil?" 93
"What is death, and why do people die?" 95

8 *Those Nasty FAQ's (Frequently Asked Questions)* 99

Matzoh Again(!?) ...or... Why Kashrut? 100
Why Can't I go to Soccer Practice...or...
    What's so special about Shabbat? 102
Where's our Christmas Tree...or...
    How Are Jews Different? 104
Why Aren't the Prayers in English...or..
    Why study Hebrew? 105
Do I really have to go to services?...or...
    Why follow rituals? 106
Why do we wear the Star of David...or...
    What is the State of Israel? 108
What is that tattoo on Uncle's arm...or...
    What was the Holocaust? 109
Why didn't Nannah go to the wedding...or...
    Why not intermarry? 110

9 *Resources & Ideas for Each Age Child* . 113

Preschool Resources 114
School-Age Resources 117
Preteen Resources 124
Teen Resources 127

10 *"F" is for Family* 131

Judaism On Parents And Parenting 133
Private Times: Between Parent and Child 135
Family Times: Collective Judaism 136
More ideas 142

11 *The Faith Profiler:Growing*
   Adult Faith..147
Determining your faith aspect 149
Adult Faith Profiler 150

12 *The Search For Understanding: The*
Path Of Intellect..153

13 *Feelings—Looking for Peace in All the*
   Right Places.. 165

14 *Friends:The Search for Relationship..175*

15 *Focus on 'Focus'* 185

   Epilogue..197

Acknowledgements

To a large degree, this book owes its existence to the many other authors whose words I have argued with, pondered over, and cherished in the past several years. To the following authors I owe much thanks: Yosef Abramowitz, Sherri Ruth Anderson, Martin Buber, Julie Hilton Danan, Hayim Halevy Donin, Patricia Hopkins, Alfred Kolatch, Harold Kushner, Lawrence Kushner, Michael Lerner, M. Scott Peck, Linda Kavelin Popov, Lesli Koppilman Ross, Jeffrey Salkin, Susan Silverman, Joseph Telushkin. Your work has done much to shape my efforts.

This book could not have been written without the help of students and others at the University of California, Irvine. I thank David G., Diane P., Josephine W., Nina K., Parysa P., and Tanya Q. for their help with interviews, and also to the sixty-some individuals who allowed themselves to be interviewed as the first glimmers of theory began to crystallize.

Many friends helped with their comments, critiques and encouraging words during the 13-plus months of hard work on this manuscript. Much thanks goes to Miriam Stein, Nannette Cohen, Barry Koff, and participants at the San Diego Writer's Conference for ideas, comments and encouraging words. Thanks to Mariska Stamenkovic for positive editing comments. Your words inspired and energized me in the long journey to the final version of this work.

And lastly and most importantly, I thank my husband Allan and daughter Claire for allowing me to ignore dirty dishes, hungry stomachs, messy desks and ringing phones to work on this project for over two years. Your patience with me allowed this work to go forward.

Introduction

*Nothing in the world is more powerful than faith.
It is the cement that holds life together. (Morris
Mandel)*

ଔ   ଔ   ଔ   ଔ   ଔ

As parents, we are given the biblical task to "train our children in the way they should go[1]", and to give them a spiritual foundation that will remain with them into adulthood. As we build this foundation, we worry that what we teach our children will be drowned out by the voices of friends and media. From the earliest age, our children are exposed to conflicting messages despite our best efforts.

I remember when I first discovered that I could not shelter my daughter from conflicting messages: she was just finishing her first week of daycare at another mother's house. I walked in, all smiles, ready to pick up my only daughter. My happiness quickly turned to surprise as I located her familiar features. She was sitting on the floor, a doll draped over her legs, hitting the doll's bottom and saying "Bad, bad girl!" Picking my jaw off the floor, I muttered something about our loud neighbors and ran out the door, embarrassed that another mom might think that, horror of horrors, I had taught my child these evil thoughts. In my bee-line to the car I glanced at another little girl, and realized that my daughter was imitating the other children who were perhaps practicing what *they* had seen other children do. As

1

I hurried home, wondering whether to change day care facilities or simply resign myself to constant sabotage, I had the sad realization that sheltering my child from society was not an option: I must learn how to deal with the barrage of negative messages.

We run into similar challenges every day. When we hear of drugs on the school grounds or children shooting children we cringe and pray to God that we can keep our children safe. We wonder how we can teach the things we believe are important, and whether our words will remain with them. Each day brings new evidence that our children don't hear what we say: after months and years of training, they *still* leave their clothes on the floor, they *don't* brush their teeth, and they *do* go out and play before they finish their homework. As the saying goes:… "gray hair is hereditary; we get it from our kids."

If it is impossible to teach a simple habit like picking up ones clothes, then how on earth are we supposed to teach our children to be good, honest, decent and faithful? And yet, if we look at adults (who are, by the way, children grown up), we see that *the greatest influence, by far, on any adult is the lessons taught to them by their parents.* Study after study shows that the values, career choices, and friendships chosen by adults are very similar to those of their parents. Messages learned as children remain with us, guiding our paths long after we leave our parents' homes. We as parents *do* make a difference in the lives of our children, and that difference lasts a lifetime.

In matters of faith, too, we can learn much about children by listening to adults. Studying adults who have remained involved with religion, I have found that there are four basic reasons that people remain faithful. Regardless whether the faith is Judaism, Catholicism, or a Protestant denomination, those who continue to remain involved do so for only four reasons:

2

- they gain understanding about their world,
- they receive a sense of comfort,
- they create a sense of relationship and connection for themselves, or
- they receive guidance for their daily lives.

These four reasons, which I have called Fact, Feeling, Friends, and Focus, have an important link to how we introduce our child to spirituality. Each of these "faith factors" is critical in creating a complete and useful faith, and needs to be introduced in a very different fashion. This book will help give your child a solid and life-long foundation in Judaism by showing you how to use the four Faith Factors to raise a spiritual child.

That I have successfully gone through seventeen years of parenting might be my most important credential for writing this book. My daughter has successfully negotiated the temptations of drugs, sex, and alcohol, is a joy to be around, and maintains above a B average in school. She has a positive outlook on life and considers herself "spiritual"; as a teen she is actively looking for a personal faith. She wants her religion to be intellectually satisfying—a particular approach to spirituality that we will examine later.

In my training as a psychologist I have worked with many families and children, giving numerous seminars on the secular aspects of parenting and discipline. My background in child development has made me aware of the importance of early input in shaping a child's path—and the vital role we parents play in developing our children's faith. For the past six years I have explored the faith histories of close to 1,000 students and community members, learning a great deal about the foundations of adult faith. Perhaps the most important insight I gained is that many decisions about religion are made very early in life. For Jews as well as others, the roots of faith are deeply embedded in the nurturing soil of the family.

Families are more than just parents and children; grandparents have an essential role to play as well. It is a lucky family that has an older generation who will spend time guiding and nurturing their grandchildren—their wisdom is important and irreplaceable. Many of the students I interviewed spoke passionately about the impact their grandmother had on their spiritual development, and many grandparents have told me of their commitment to instill a love of Judaism in their grandchildren. This book is as much for grandparents as it is for parents—both parties have valuable lessons to teach.

The ideas presented here are based on extensive research, but that is not the reason I recommend them. I recommend them because they work. I have seen people apply them successfully over and over again. I've heard from people who have used the ideas without knowing the underlying theory—and they still work. I know without a doubt that the Faith Factors can help *you* to raise children who value spirituality and will maintain their ties to the Jewish community throughout their days.

Within these pages are three tools to help you along this path. First, you will find descriptions and explanations of the four "faith factors", as well as helpful guidance to find your child's primary factor. There are also extensive lists of resources and suggestions for children and families: literally hundreds of ideas for growing your child's faith. And lastly, separate chapters contain ideas for adults to grow their own faith, to provide strong examples for their children to follow.

    ೞ   ೞ   ೞ   ೞ   ೞ

As parents we are in the ideal position to guide and nurture our child's spirituality, by helping them hild find his or her own path to a personally fulfilling Judaism. Raising a spiritual child, like gardening, requires constant attention and loving care. But the beautiful roses and solid oaks that blossom after years of care and feeding are more than payment in full. As you prepare to break ground for this exciting task, this book will be your guide.

1
"What's a Parent to Do?"

Faith is the material that will not shrink when washed in the tears of affliction. Living without faith is like driving a car without headlights on a moonless and starless night. (Morris Mandel)

ଔ   ଔ   ଔ   ଔ   ଔ

Putting God in the Picture

The greatest reward of parenting is the pride we take in our children once they have grown. You can always tell the parents who feel this pride; ask about their child and their face lights up, their voice changes, and they talk about their son or daughter for five minutes without pause. As a parent with a child still at home, I see these parents as role models. One of the most valuable lessons they have shown me is the importance of providing children with a sense of purpose, with a foundation for their lives.

Psychologist Victor Frankl says that each person has an inborn desire to find a meaning for his or her existence—a central purpose that creates meaning in the events that continually swirl around us[2]. If we don't choose spirituality as that foundation, our choices are meager.

"You can never be too rich or too thin," says one pop

phrase, encouraging us to pursue wealth and physical beauty as our guiding forces. As lonely millionaires and anorexic teens can attest, reaching these goals creates a hollow victory. Other value systems encourage becoming "top dog": getting the biggest commission, the best house, the newest video equipment. These accomplishments create excitement in the short term, but in the long term leave us asking, "is that all there is?"

As a foundation for living, faith and spirituality cannot be surpassed. We, as parents and grandparents, know that faith provides direction in stressful times, assistance in every-day decisions, and solutions to daily problems. Spirituality can give our sons and daughters a central focus when friends, advertisements, and other enticements threaten to divert their attention. As parents, we can give no greater gift than that of a spiritual center that guides and protects our children. Introducing our children to faith early on makes God the prime candidate to become the foundation for life.

It is our main task as parents to grow responsible adults—to "train them in the way they should go." In raising a child to spirituality, we provide him or her with the tools necessary for continued growth and a sense of purpose that cannot be found anywhere else. If we want to raise children to be proud of, we as parents need to provide them with the best possible foundation: we need to put God in the picture.

*When the people of Israel stood at Mount Sinai
ready to receive the Torah, God said to them,
"Bring me proof that you will cherish it, and then
I will give the Torah to you."*

*They said, "Our ancestors will be our proof."
Said God to them, "I have faults to find with your
ancestors, they are not proof enough. But bring
Me some other assurance and I will give it to*

you."

*They said, "King of the Universe, our prophets
will be our proof." He replied, "I have faults to
find with your prophets also."*

*They said to Him, "Then, our children will be
our proof." God smiled in his heart and replied,
"Indeed, your children are excellent proof. For
their sake I will give you the Torah."
(adapted from Song of Songs Rabbah 1:4)*

೮ଷ   ೮ଷ   ೮ଷ   ೮ଷ   ೮ଷ

A Call to the Heart

But what *is* this thing called spirituality? It seems to be the
word of the decade—"I'm not religious, but I'm spiritual" we
hear over and over again (and perhaps you have said it yourself).
If being spiritual is so important, what is this thing that we're
striving to be? There are probably as many answers as there are
"spiritual" people, but the common thread is a call to the heart.
Spirituality is an inward pulling of God to our very center,
making God a part of who we are. To be spiritual means striving
to live day-to-day in the manner God expects of us, using our
faith as a grid over the chaos of life.

Spirituality is more than knowing the beliefs and values
of one's faith. The commitment to spirituality *is above and
beyond* the doctrines and beliefs we claim as our own. These
beliefs themselves are critical to faith—we cannot have faith
without embracing core doctrines and values. But spirituality is
the emotional and behavioral reaction *to* these beliefs: one
cannot be spiritual without having it affect word and deed.

Religion only becomes spirituality when we take it out of

9

the prayerbook and bring it into our daily life. When we use the values of our faith with our boss and coworkers, in the supermarket, and with our families, we shift from being a "religious" person to being a truly spiritual being. We declare ourselves to have an internal commitment to faith, and decide that from then on, it will guide our lives. Spirituality enriches and transforms our lives. Once we have experienced it, we can't wait to pass this precious gift on to our children. Luckily, children can make a similar shift to spirituality. But for that 'shift' to be possible, the concepts they learn and stories they memorize have to take on a personal meaning, creating the desire to follow God.

When I was in grade school, my mother had an impressive garden. She loved her garden and enjoyed tending it; she planted, fertilized, and pulled weeds with a vengeance. I would help her when she asked, but inwardly I groaned every time she held out the gardening gloves. I loved my mother, but I didn't like sitting in the sun, and the clippers hurt my hand. Her garden just didn't mean all that much to me.

After I moved out of the house as a college student, I went on to kill every houseplant I was given. My first attempts at outdoor gardening were no more successful; the apartments were rented, and I had no real ownership of the soil. So I'd plant things, "forget" to water them, and they'd die. My mother was appalled: "I thought I taught you better than that!" She had, but something just hadn't clicked. But things changed dramatically when I bought my first home. I bought every garden book written, installed sprinklers myself (so the watering couldn't be forgotten) and soon I had a small but impressive garden. What happened? I had ownership. The soil and its contents were totally mine.

In the same way, our children need "ownership" of Judaism to create their own personal religious meaning—to become spiritual. They need to bring it close to their hearts and

10

feel it call to them individually. Like the earth, religion needs to be cupped it in our hands, and held close so we can say "this is mine, and mine alone." To help our children become spiritual beings, we need to give them a sense of ownership of their faith.

Yes, We Can!

> *What God is to the world, parents are to their children. (Philo)*
>
> ೞ   ೞ   ೞ   ೞ   ೞ

It would be marvelous if there were a Spirituality Counselor in every junior high and high school who could help us show our children the importance of faith. "Well James," the counselor would say, "you've scored well on your exams, but it seems that you haven't attended many Shabbat services lately. Let's put in some more work on that area. Faith needs work just like your academics, and we want to excel, now, don't we?" This scenario will never happen in the public schools, and even religious schools don't do much in this respect.

Neither do our children see examples of faith in society at large. We are bombarded on all sides by messages that focus on money, looks, strength, and power. Is there advertising that suggests that we be moral, kind to our fellows, or give charity (*tzedakah*)? Rarely. How many network television programs emphasize turning to God, using religious values, or using your congregation for social activities? Very few. This leaves the task of raising spiritual children up to us, the family.

The family's role in raising a spiritual child has never been more important. In earlier times society was a valuable partner in child-rearing, but those days are over. Nowadays, family is the single most influential source of guidance for their children. Sociologists often describe the task of teaching cultural values as a "three-legged stool" approach, the three legs being

11

family, society, and religious institutions. This hypothetical stool is badly crippled (if not altogether destroyed) if one of the legs fails to hold up. This scenario is playing out today: society, or community, is failing to "hold up its end" and the stool is clearly wobbling, threatening to spill our children into the world unprepared and without the foundation they desperately need. Since community has ceased to support the teaching of values, it becomes essential that the remaining two legs of the stool—family and religious institutions—join forces to prevent disaster. By unifying their efforts to become one solid pedestal, faith and family can keep the this pedestal of values upright to support our children. The role of parents is crucial in forming a strong union in which family can bolster faith, while faith bolsters the family.

A perfect example of this strong bond is given by one college student whose aunt was fighting a battle with cancer. "When she was in the hospital" she writes, "my aunt would ask us to pray for her. We'd gather around the bed and pray for a long time. I wasn't used to praying like that, so it felt pretty strange at first. But she wanted us to do it, so we did. Later, we started praying by ourselves even outside of the hospital." Even though the aunt did succumb to the disease, Karla goes on to say "my aunt's trust in us absolutely strengthened my faith. Without my aunt asking, I never would have said daily prayers. Now, I do it whenever I can." Karla's aunt showed her an example of faith, from which the entire family drew the strength to deal with the aunt's eventual death.

As parents, we don't need to start from scratch when we introduce our children to faith; children have a natural inclination towards spirituality. Especially in the younger years, they have an inborn sense of the magical that is very close to the sacred. When young Jeffrey writes, "Dear God, It is great the way you always get the stars in the right places[3]," he touches on the mystical-magical ideas of God that come so naturally to

12

children. Families, too, often have special moments that naturally lead to spiritual feelings. When your son makes his first soccer goal, or your granddaughter solos in the school's spring concert, the swell you feel in your heart is a short step away from giving thanks to God for the gift we have been given. These moments are the beginnings of family-based spirituality.

It's perhaps easier for Jewish families to provide this guidance than it is for others. For the 1500 years since the destruction of the temple in Jerusalem, the home has been the center of Jewish life. Much of Judaism's ritual and celebration takes place in the home, making family a natural source of religious guidance. Parents who rely only on religious institutions to instill a sense of spirituality face an uphill battle: they must take the "one size fits all" religious curriculum and hope it fits the very unique needs of their child. When spirituality begins at home, parents can create their own unique and personal ways to celebrate the joy and richness of their Jewish heritage.

When you decide to bring faith into your child's lives, the task may seem awkward and tremendously confusing. But if you look back on learning to drive a car (or ride a bicycle), it probably seemed the same. Practice, repetition, and a commitment to succeed are the most important tools for success, and parents are in the very best position to use them. To paraphrase the words of Rabbi Hillel, the famous Jewish sage, "If not us, who? And if not now, when?"

> *We are given children to test us and to make us*
> *more spiritual. (George F. Will)*

03   03   03   03   03

But how do we show our children and grandchildren this path, and which tools, exactly, do we use? More importantly, how can we be certain that what children learn today will stay with them into adulthood? We need help to find the right path for our child. There *is* a way to navigate through the hundreds of books on parenting and dozens of teaching methods to find a match with our child's specific needs. Using the faith benefits— Fact, Feeling, Friends, and Focus—you and your child will forge strong bonds to Judaism built to last a lifetime. The resources contained in this book are matched to your child's personal needs, allowing you to guide him or her along the road to inner faith. Raising a spiritual child *is* possible; you have in your hands a guide for the journey.

Cஐ   Cஐ   Cஐ   Cஐ   Cஐ

2
The Four Factors of Faith

*Genuine religious movements do not seek to offer
man the solution to the mystery of the world, they
seek to equip him to live through the power of
that mystery; they do not seek to teach him about
the nature of God but to show him the path where
he can encounter God. (Martin Buber)*

CB   CB   CB   CB   CB

Discovering the Faith Factors

Faith is a powerful motivation. Because of it, people have
sacrificed love, health, and even life. Faith plays a crucial role
for thousands, even millions of people—people from all walks of
life, some as different as day and night. How can faith become a
compelling force that continues from childhood into adulthood?
More importantly: How can parents raise *their* child to embrace
faith in their adult lives? This is the question my University of
California research team wanted to answer. So I spoke with
hundreds of individuals across the United States[4], looking for
answers to that very question. I asked old and young, Jews,
Christians, and those with no affiliation. I did not know what the
answers would reveal, I just knew that the answer could only be

found by talking to individuals who *lived* their faith.

As religion was an important factor in my own life, I also thought hard about these issues from a personal perspective, and spoke to many friends who were spiritually inclined. In all of this asking, talking, and thinking I discovered many truths, among which was that people love talking about their faith. Many times, when I set interview appointments people insisted on brief meetings because they had "other things to do". Then as we got to the end of the structured questions and the end of the tape, they would invite me to say longer and offer to call in their spouses or parents. Even those who rated themselves a "6" on a 1-10 scale of religiosity would remark how enjoyable our conversations had been. I, too, felt uplifted after each interview. I would leave feeling as though I had been in the honored presence of something very special; each person had allowed me to see a glimpse of their soul.

These interviews and responses, resulting in hundreds of stories and suggestions, led to an exciting discovery. We expected to find a plethora of reasons for people to become and remain involved with their faith, reasons that differed for children and adults. But from over 400 individuals, we did not find 400 different reasons. Instead we found only four. Regardless of religious affiliation and age, people commit to their faith for **four basic reasons**.

Interestingly, these benefits appeared in each religious tradition I examined—from Evangelical Christian to Reform Judaism to Mormonism. Although the remainder of this chapter speaks in the language of Judaism, it could just as well be discussing Presbyterian faith or the Roman Catholic tradition. The four reasons or "aspects" uncovered by this research reach beyond doctrine and beliefs, touching the essence of faith itself. The aspects show four benefits that people receive from their spiritual practices: to *understand* their world, to *feel comforted* and protected, to *feel connected* to others, or to *receive guidance* in their daily lives. We called these factors <u>Fact</u>, <u>Feeling</u>, <u>Friends</u>, and <u>Focus</u>.

Facts—The Search for Understanding

We all want to understand our world, to make sense of what goes on around us, and understand why we are here. When we turn to religion to answer these questions, we focus on the intellectual aspects of faith. We apply reason to our beliefs, and evaluate our lives using a framework of spirituality. People driven chiefly by their search for understanding have a specific orientation to their faith—an orientation we call FACT.

The rabbis of old believed Torah study to be the most sacred ritual of Jewish life. These fathers who created the Talmud with its logical discussions of the fine points of *halakhah* (Jewish law) were practicing the aspect of Fact. By bringing order and understanding into Jewish life, they created the intellectual tradition that is central to Judaism today.

We gathered many childhood recollections from the interviews that were direct reflections of this faith factor. Several students mentioned that religion made sense of things when they were children—that through the aspect of Fact, a grandparent's death or a parent's illness was understandable. Other adults were drawn towards in-depth study of scriptures and discussions with others in their congregations.

Adults satisfy this search for facts by attending lectures, seminars and courses, going to Bible study classes, and looking for a congregation where the Shabbat *D'var Torah* is thought-provoking. In children (especially of school age), Fact is seen in the hundreds of questions that are asked about faith, ranging from why God created fleas, to the meaning of the Jonah story, to the importance of a particular holiday.

Feeling—the Search for Comfort

Most of us at some point have feelings of love, comfort, and personal fulfillment during religious experiences. The aspect of emotion allows us to involve our core being in our faith, opening us to a sense of being surrounded by God. This is the aspect of emotion, or FEELINGS. Those people drawn to Feelings told us that their faith gave them a sense of being loved, at peace, and cared for. Childhood stories we heard included numerous accounts of feeling safe, knowing that "God is looking down on me."

The teachings and tradition of the Kabbalistic tradition demonstrate the Feelings perspective. The Kabbalists looked for direct, intense experiences of holiness, which are clearly emotional experiences. Although they were certainly not anti-intellectual, the early Kabbalists would say that intellect (Fact) is merely a gateway to the real thing: the emotional experience of God's presence.

Adults who were drawn to this factor pointed out two main sources for their comfort. The first was communion with God through prayer or meditation; many mentioned feeling at peace, knowing that God was there to comfort and understand them. Weekly worship services provide another common source of comfort and positive feelings. Adults often mention feeling safe and peaceful when they worship with others, giving rise to a sense of being "in the hands of God." For children, too, attendance at worship services brings forth strong feelings and positive emotions.

Friends—The Search for Relationship

We are by nature social beings, and what could be more basic than having a "relationship" with our Creator? Through this factor, we form a connection with God, his messengers, and

18

other individuals who share our spiritual commitment to bring God into everyday life. The word that describes this aspect's essence is FRIENDS.

Martin Buber wrote eloquently about a relationship with God by emphasizing that God "enters into a direct relationship with us men in creative, revealing, and redeeming acts, and thus makes it possible for us to enter into a direct relationship with Him[5]." The many of us who join *havurot* (plural of *havurah*) enjoy the aspect of Friends through making Judaism part of our social activities.

Adults who gravitate towards this spiritual emphasis enjoy being with others who are religious. More than just a social gathering, interaction with others within their faith gives people a feeling that they are part of something larger than themselves. Children also enjoy being a part of a group, and often hold more than one childhood memory of a special trip or summer camp where a special connection to others (and God) was formed. As adults we gain a sense of relationship through attending congregational social events or forming small groups with other like-minded families. These positive feelings are passed on to our children, who enjoy play groups with other congregant families or outings with family friends.

Focus—the Search for Guidance

We all need a set of guidelines to show us how to make those important decisions of life (and even the not-so-important ones!). Our faith provides an important resource for these rules and standards, giving us direction and guidance in our daily affairs. This is the path of FOCUS.

Jews have a corner on the guidance market: there are 613 expectations for us to follow! When Maimonides[6] proclaimed that there was a commandment for every day of the year and part of the body (hence the total 613) he created a powerful connection between Judaism and the path of Focus. The strong Jewish ethical tradition also provides important guidelines, making yet another way in which faith can provide guidance and direction.

In our research we heard many childhood stories describing prayers to God for help or to "fix" things—to heal their grandparents or help with grades in school. Adults, too, often spoke of looking to God or their clergy for direction. Those emphasizing Focus (the largest group we found in our research) looks for counsel on important issues and guidance in daily life. Through the aspect of Focus, faith provides guidance in these important moments.

Adults find this guidance by following positive role models, attending Bible studies, or discussing dilemmas with spiritual leaders. Gradeschool children naturally gravitate towards this aspect of faith; regular religious school can assist them in their search for clear direction and guidance.

The Balance of "Four"

The symbolism of the number four recurs in many faith traditions, mirroring the quartet of paths we found. In Native American religions, the four-part medicine wheel is a powerful symbol, each quadrant representing a different spiritual path. Hinduism also recognizes four paths to enlightenment and four faces of Brahma, the creator-god. In Christianity, four-fold symbols usually refer to divinity, combining the familiar trinity (the three-part God, Son and Holy Spirit) with the "God within" that links us to God. Important Jewish symbols also contain four parts: the *Zohar* (Judaism's mystical text) speaks of four worlds between ourselves and God, and the four-letter tetragrammaton (YHVH) forms the unpronounceable name of God.

In daily life we deal with four points of the compass, four seasons, four stages of life. The number four has its own

20

symmetry and balance that implies completeness; just so, the four paths described here complement each other and create a complete faith. One must use all four aspects of faith—understanding, emotion, connection, and guidance—to create a whole faith.

All four faith benefits (understanding, comfort, connection and guidance) are critical parts of a complete spirituality. We need *understanding*, gained through study and discussion, to understand life's important issues. The *comfort* we receive through knowing God's concern for us provides us with a sense of safety as we progress through life. Faith cannot be experienced fully without a *connection* to others of similar mind, and spiritual values provide the *direction* that we certainly need. Just as a house of worship needs more than one wall, we need all four areas to create a strong link to our faith.

Which Aspect for Whom?

> *Every person born into the world represents*
> *something new; something that never existed*
> *before, something original and unique. (Martin*
> *Buber)*

CB   CB   CB   CB   CB

The adults we interviewed told us two things about these aspects of faith. First, that their "preferred" factor of faith changed as they progressed through life. What interested them at one time was replaced later by another aspect of faith. We saw this pattern with children also; younger children were drawn to different dimensions of faith than were older children and teens. Secondly, most people did not know why they chose a particular factor. "It just seemed right," one 60-year-old Catholic gentleman said. As humans we respond to the call of religion in an almost unconscious manner, but certainly not without reason. In fact, there are several good reasons: our personality, our stage of life, our family, and our culture.

Our personalities: There are just about as many personalities as there are people; each of us is unique in the ways we act, react, and interact with others. But there are basic patterns that we can all recognize: extroverted types, analytical types, warm-fuzzy personalities, and so on. There is definite overlap between a personality and the faith factor that holds most appeal.   For example, those of us that enjoy analysis can become quite interested in theological arguments, finding our deepest faith in Fact, the aspect of intellect. Those who are extroverted and enjoy the company of others may be naturally drawn to experience faith through the factor of relationship: Friends. The faith aspect of Emotion is attractive to those who are more emotional by nature, and Focus is most appealing to those who seek structure in their lives.

Looking at any bar or bat mitzvah you can see this principle at work. The boys and girls who are out in the middle of the dance floor the entire time are most likely the extroverts who will be drawn to the Friends factor. Those who sit at the tables and talk are probably more likely to emphasize the Focus or Facts element of faith. And those who seems to sit back and take it all in are likely drawn to Feelings. These parallels can be quite striking, although as we shall see they clearly interact with other parts of life, such as the stage of life—school-age, young adulthood, and so on.

Our life stage: The statement "life is what happens when we are making other plans" underscores the fact that life is constantly changing. As one stage of our life blends into the next— pursuing education or job promotions, finding mates, raising children—our priorities shift almost without our notice. This fact was echoed over and over in the adults we interviewed. We found that one typical pattern was to become very concerned with the needs of children in the elementary school and middle school years, and then to shift the focus to the adult's needs when children moved away. Into retirement, the primary need was for friends, and thus the aspect of relationship. Said Susan, a Jewish woman in her late 50's, "When I had young kids, the synagogue had other parents that we did things with. I got Jewish friends and so did my children. When the kids got older, I started thinking about my own needs. I wanted more Jewish knowledge, so we changed synagogues to one that had more study groups. Now, I really like the services. They give me a sense of shalom—peace." This story and others like it show that religion does meet many needs for each of us. Faith can and does grow with us as we change.

Children, too, change their emphasis as they grow. The next chapter describes this process in more detail, but one comment from Jerry, now 19, illustrates the point. "I used to go to Shabbat services just to be with my parents. Now, I go because it makes me feel good." This provides yet another reason to introduce a child to all four faith benefits: the factor that is the least important today may become the most important ten years from now.

> *When Mother Theresa received the Nobel Peace Prize, she was asked, "What can we do to promote world peace?" She replied, "Go home and love your family."*
>
> ␣ଓ␣␣␣␣ଓ␣␣␣␣ଓ␣␣␣␣ଓ␣␣␣␣ଓ

Our families: Parents remain one of the most influential forces well into our adult years. As adults, we often wonder what our parents would think of our activities, and most of us (I can't be the only one…) revert to the role we had as children when we pay our parents a visit. The ways in which our family practiced their religion (or didn't practice it) have great impact on adult faith. But even more important than what we *did* as children was how we *felt* when we did it. Acts that made us feel good we return to; those that made us feel bad, we avoid. So the religious and spiritual acts we enjoyed with our families, whether it was Sukkot picnics, Passover dinners, or singing during services, we usually continue doing. If our families enjoyed the social and relationship-building parts of their faith, we are likely to do the same. If they enjoyed learning about religious concepts, we often carry that preference with us into adulthood.

A very non-Jewish story about cooking and families comes to mind to describe this generation-to-generation transference. A newly married woman was fixing her husband his first ham (you could change it to a corned beef, but the story just wouldn't be the same.) She unpackaged the ham, cut off both ends, and stuck it in the pan. "Why do you cut off the ends?" asked the husband. "My mother always did it that way," replied the bride. "She said it was more tender." The next time they had ham at her mother's house, he asked again. "Why do you cut off the ends?" "Oh, I don't know," said the mother. "*My* mother always cooked it that way, and she made great ham." So, the next time they gathered at the grandmother's house, the husband was determined to get to the bottom of the mystery. "Granny," he said, "why do you cut the ends off of the ham before you cook it?" "My heavens", said the grandmother. "I haven't done that in years. I used to have a small oven, and cutting off the ends was the only way I could fit it in the pan!" Traditions get passed down through generations, and sometimes the original reason is lost. But family traditions are comforting, and going back to what we know (whether it's food for our bodies or food for our souls) is a gratifying experience.

Our culture: Culture is a term we use to describe

many different aspects of our lives. It can mean the food we eat, the holidays we celebrate, the clothes we wear. Here, however, we are speaking of our religious culture—the indications of what is spiritually expected or "normal." Our congregations, our communities, even our countries can give us messages about the correct ways to "do religion." Take a look at your own religious culture:

- What holidays do Jews (or Christians or Moslems) in the community take off from work?
- How often do most people attend worship services?
- What dietary restrictions are observed by most Jews in the community?
- What religious publications does your community read?

All of these pieces of culture show us the "expected" way to worship and use our faith. As adults, we make decisions about whether to follow these expectations or make our own way. But for children, cultural expectations are particularly strong influences; very few children willingly go against the "cultural norm" and choose their own path.

> *Faith is...knowing there is an ocean, because you have seen a brook; a mountain, because you have seen a hill; God, because you have seen man.*
> *(Morris Mandel)*

     ߚ   ߚ   ߚ   ߚ   ߚ

These influences—personality, stage of life, family, and culture—combine in myriad ways to create a personal "spiritual reward system" and draw us to one of the four rewards of faith: understanding, comfort, connection, or guidance. For each child and adult there will be one area that will create the strongest link to faith. Finding your child's unique spiritual reward system will reveal the path to **your** child's personal relationship with his or her faith—and thus to spirituality. How parents, grandparents and caregivers can find the most important benefit for each child is discussed in the next chapter. Through looking at developmental stage, personality and preferred activities, and family factors, you can find the best way to lead each child on a personal path to spirituality.

CB   CB   CB   CB   CB

3
Watching our Children Grow

Loving a child is a circular business. The more you give, the more you get; the more you get, the more you give. (Penelope Leach)

ଓ   ଓ   ଓ   ଓ   ଓ

Children are amazingly complex creatures. One of the joys of parenting is when a son or daughter does something totally unexpected, and we beam with pride at their surprising accomplishment. We watch with wonder as our tiny charges grow physically, mentally and emotionally to become our equals (well, almost our equals). Some of the developmental changes we see are hard-wired and happen automatically: physical growth, increased strength, and advanced language skills usually happen without much input from others. But other areas such as establishing a moral code, developing values or growing in faith depend more on outside influences. Families, friends, schools, and society at large all provide input to this important area.

Parents and others who want to have a strong influence on the development of a child's faith can use a "Child Development 101" refresher, especially as it regards how children understand their world and how their objectives change as they grow. This chapter provides a roadmap (complete with signposts) for adults watching a child march down the path to adulthood. Regardless of your child's age, you will find helpful information here on what is, and what is to come.

Of Piaget and Erikson

Children's ability to think, or *cognitive level*, was described in the 1950s by psychologist Jean Piaget who developed his theory by watching his three daughters grow up. He found that the thinking of a preschooler has fundamental differences from the style of a school-aged child, who also thinks very differently from a teenager. While that fact may seem obvious to even the most casual observer, Piaget was the first to *describe* these differences in a way that showed the progression from stage to stage. The specifics of these styles of thinking, called preconventional reasoning, concrete operations, and formal operations, are described in the chart below.

Eric Erikson was also a pioneer in the study of development, describing a process he called *psychosocial development.* He described a different challenge to be met in each stage of life from infancy to old age, for a total of seven psychosocial stages. Each stage presented a challenge to be faced that he described as a pair of opposite outcomes. Each person either successfully conquers the challenge and moves to the next level, or stays mired in one developmental level trying to resolve the issue (listed in the chart below). If this explanation sounds Freudian to you, give yourself two points. Erikson studied with Freud for a time before designing his own new-and-improved theory that eliminated the sexual issues. Each stage has its own goal, beginning with preschoolers who are striving to create autonomy for themselves. Children who can't accomplish this task are destined to feel a sense of guilt. Likewise, school-age children are looking for a sense of accomplishment without

28

which they feel inferior; preteens look for peer acceptance if they are to avoid feeling alienated, and teens seek personal identity to avoid a sense of confusion.

Areas of Development

Age Group	Cognitive Level (Piaget)	Psychosocial Task (Erikson)
Preschool	Preconventional reasoning: Uses magical thinking (fantasy and reality are mixed); sees only own perspective.	Initiative vs. guilt: Explores to find out consequences (pushes buttons). Looks for stability in outside world. Goal: a separate identity from parents.
School-age	Concrete operations: Can give logical explanations for events; grasps difference between fantasy & reality, sees other perspectives	Industry vs. inferiority. Learns new skills, discovers personal abilities. Learns to compare and self-evaluate. Goal: a sense of personal accomplishment
Pre-teen	(Transition to formal operations): some abstract thinking skills.	Group Identity vs. Alienation. Chooses groups to identify with. Learns to deal with peer pressure. Goal: peer acceptance
Teen	Formal operations: Can look at possibilities for the future, follow sequence of events to its logical conclusion, finds logical inconsistencies	Identity vs. identity confusion. Determines own path through life, finds comfortable peer group. Goal: a personal identity

Using these theories of cognitive and psychosocial development, James Fowler created a theory of faith development. He interviewed hundreds of children and adults asking about fate, purpose, and the meaning of life and found (not surprisingly) that as we mature, our perceptions of God do as well. As children go from preschool to elementary school through the pre-teen years and on to become teenagers, their perceptions of the world, themselves, and God change tremendously. When we understand these different viewpoints, we can become more effective at teaching our children and grandchildren about faith.

The Religious World of Preschoolers

"Can you tell me what God looks like?"
"He has a light shirt on, he has brown hair, he had brown eyelashes"
"Does everybody think God looks like that?"
"Mmm—not when he gets a haircut."
(from Stages of Faith, by James Fowler, 1981).

The world of a four-year-old is a mix of reality and fantasy, causing us to stop in our tracks listening to some of their more colorful ideas. Said one adult who I interviewed, "I used to think bananas fell from the sky instead of growing on trees. I guess I got it mixed up with 'manna' in the desert and coconuts that were always hitting people on the head. I still eat lots of bananas—they somehow seem special." This style of thinking is a mixture of stories, movies, and reality, and creates strong images that can last into adulthood. These images are also laden with emotion: preschoolers who hear stories of a loving God hold onto this picture into adulthood. Those who know of God as demanding and judgmental retain a severe image of God.

Preschoolers are extremely responsive to images and

pictures. The best way to create a lasting impression on a preschooler is to give him a strong image. They enjoy stories, and even though they cannot repeat them scene for scene, they remember the images well into adulthood (as we can see from the banana example above.) Three and four-year-olds don't understand that others can have a different perspective from their own; their image of God, they believe, is everyone else's as well. For them, God is mostly a policeman making sure that people behave as they should. As they seek to find their own limits, they see religion as a set of rules governing simple behaviors (you should go to synagogue, you should not hit your sister). Other, more complex ideas come later—when they find out there are many ways to bend society's rules.

Children in this age group are very interested in hearing stories about their faith. Picture books are wonderful for this age group, for children will keep a visual memory long after the books have seen their last days. Action-packed epics like David and Goliath, or problem-solving tales (about King Solomon's court, for example,) are stories that will stick in the minds of these children for many years.

One Jewish educator I know tells the story of taking his three-year-old daughter to the beach. After playing for some time in the sand, she collected three sticks and planted two of them in the ground. With the third, she touched the tops of the two upright pillars, mumbling something he could not quite hear. "What are you doing?" her father asked. "I'm making Shabbat," she replied. Her recollection of the Shabbat candle-lighting ceremony reveals the importance of ritual in the preschool years. Preschoolers yearn for stability in a world that seems to be blossoming with new discoveries every day. Religious rituals create a sense of comfort; all is well when the same steps are repeated with daily or weekly regularity.

For this age group, the most relevant faith factor involves

the social aspect—the factor of Friends. The best way to integrate younger children into a faith community is for the parents to be active with their Jewish friends. If you have preschoolers, your friends probably have preschoolers also. Be sure the families get together regularly, and encourage the kids to play together often. Temples, too, cater to preschool families with "Torah Tot" programs and the like. Find a program with an active parent group, and you may find yourself another set of blossoming friendships!

Spirituality in Elementary School

Dear God,
How come you didn't invent any new animals lately? We still have just all the old ones. Johny. *(from Children's Letters to God: The New Collection)*

Children in elementary school rarely employ the vivid and colorful language we find in preschoolers. Now they clearly can see what is real and what is fantasy and (thank you very much) they are most *certainly* not interested in fantasy. Elementary school can be a very serious time, when your fanciful preschooler becomes aware of the important (and *very* serious) ideas that he will need to learn. Don't worry, the sense of playfulness usually returns sometime in the teens. There are still many things they don't know, but they tend to fill in blank areas with their best guesses instead of imagined truths. Children in this age group are working hard to succeed, meeting the goals set by teachers, parents, and themselves. At this point, religion begins to be about morality and rules, gathered mostly from stories. Their images of God are still fairly impersonal; God is "up there" looking at us "down here" and is definitely in charge:

"How does (God) rule the world?"

32

*"Well, he—not really rule the world, but um—
let's see, he like—he lives on top of the world and
he's watching over everybody. At least he tries to.
And he does what he thinks is right." (from
Stages of Faith, by James Fowler.)*

Children at this age begin to make religion part of their own belief systems. Those lucky enough to have a foundation in faith can begin to form a spiritual view of the world, even if their views are based on a very literal and one-dimensional view of faith (God, for example, is very likely seen as an all-loving rabbi-in-the-sky). While they can begin to understand that there are other viewpoints in the world, they are clear that "this one is mine", and they will hold onto it firmly in the face of significant opposition.

Children in this age group are capable of remembering tremendous amounts of facts, and religious school becomes a natural addition to their weekly schedule when their capacity for Jewish history and Hebrew outstrips their parents' ability to feed them information. Families benefit, too, from meeting other Jewish children and families who become part of your social network (not to mention carpool buddies!).

For most children in elementary school, guidance (the factor of Focus) creates the primary connection to faith. Their major goal is to learn *what* the guidelines are, but not necessarily *why*. Although your nine- or ten-year-old can be excited about learning a list of rules such as the Ten Commandments, he doesn't yet have the skills to explain the reasons behind them. (Give that task to his teenage sister—she'd probably enjoy the challenge.) Morality and moral decision-making become issues in the elementary years, and introducing children to Jewish ethics—another aspect of Focus— is a natural at this age.

God in the Middle School Years

Dear God,

I feel very near to you. I feel like you are beside me all the time. Please be with me on Thursday. I am running in a 3 mile race then. I will need all the speed in the world. If you are not busy with other things, maybe you could be at the starting line, the finish line, and everywhere in between. Frankie, age 11 *(from Dear God: Children's Letters to God)*

Preteens are definitely in a transitional time; they do not want to be considered "kids", but have not yet earned the right to be among their idols, the teens. Their faith, too, is in transition. For the most part their understanding of God is identical to the views they formed in elementary school, yet they crave a more personal relationship with God. One adult remembered an episode from when she was 12 that epitomizes this desire. She tells the story of sitting on her bed, feeling sorry for herself and sending a heartfelt prayer to God saying, "God, if you care about me, show me some sign". She says that she did have a mystical experience as a result of her prayer, proving to her that God cared about her personally. She says "then and there I decided that God was real and that He cared about *me*—not just people in general." Preteens need a personally-relevant God, not merely a deity sitting on some far-off cloud.

Preteens begin to question the literal interpretations they took for granted as younger children. Their intellectual skills are sharpening, and they realize that many ideas are deeper than they had imagined before. At the same time they are very concerned with "fitting in", and finding the correct group of friends becomes a major project. For parents, this creates an excellent opportunity to encourage Jewish friendships. Developing a Jewish peer group increases the chances that preteens will dig deeper into religion. Without this focus, they are content to ignore serious religious analysis for a time; they'd much rather discuss the latest movies, hairstyles, or decide who is a "fox" or "too cool".

The preteen years are a critical time for Jewish youth, as it comes immediately before bar or bat mitzvah. If you are lucky enough to find a strong Hebrew school with many youngsters of the same age, you may find that your child gravitates towards this group for a time. This group can help strengthen the connection to Judaism and solidify the idea of faith as a natural part of life. Others may not be so fortunate; their child may turn instead to another peer group (soccer team-mates or neighbors, for example). In this case, the family can provide extra support to create the strong Jewish connection that will last into adulthood.

The personalities of middle school youth are just beginning to crystallize, hence the factor to which they are most drawn depends on personal inclination. For many (boys especially) the factor of Fact is most interesting. They are intrigued by the possibility of knowing more about their faith, and their developing intellect can grasp the more difficult concepts that they couldn't understand a few years earlier. The aspect of Fact allows them to understand life from a spiritual perspective, creating a solid foundation for the future. For many girls, a sense of comfort and/or safety are important links to faith (the aspect of Feelings). Making a connection with God through daily prayer and through participation in weekly services will strengthen this bond.

The aspect of Friends is particularly strong at this age for boys *and* girls. Jewish groups are particularly important at this time, and (as we mentioned before) a congregation with a strong youth program is an important addition to help grow personal faith. Friendships that begin here can have a lasting impact and strengthen your child's link to faith even more.

Faith in the Teen Years

*"How important do you think your parents'
influence has been (in deciding your beliefs)?"*

*"My parents have guided me in the right
direction...I'm glad that they've done what
they've done. They've taught me to do the right
from wrong and everything, and I've taken it from
there. From what I know...They brought me to
(synagogue) and taught me about God and love
and everything, and now I know what it is and..
and I'll be telling* my *daughter or my son, or
whatever, the same thing." (from Stages of Faith,
by James Fowler)*

Many parents think that spirituality in teens is a non-existent; at this point, their ideas are set and no more input is possible. Quite the contrary! A teen's primary goal is to create a personal identity that includes an over-arching philosophy of life; faith and spirituality are prime candidates for this job. But the faith they require is a much fuller version than that required by their ten-year-old sister. Their new reasoning skills let them see logical inconsistencies, in fact they *live* to find illogical statements—especially when made by someone in authority! (Never argue with a teen—they usually win due to sheer tenacity.)

The lives of adolescents are complex: teens have responsibilities to family and school, perhaps to a job, to their peers and to society. If Judaism is to serve as a guiding force it must speak to all of these different areas, giving a sense of unity to these seemingly unconnected demands. Judaism can serve as the focal point of a teen's life, but it takes a commitment from both the teen and his parents to make Judaism this core concept. Teens can and do mold to the expectations of their parents in this respect; parents who have a full sense of their religion's value, or who can provide it through their congregation, have the greatest success in forming a bond between their teen and Judaism.

Teens look for role models, and the presence of a respected rabbi or other religious leader is important to them. Many teens turn to these leaders before looking to their parents for religious guidance. If you are active in your congregation, the chances that your teen will choose a Jewish role model are increased. But even with positive Jewish role models, many teens decide for a time that they are going to be Buddhist (or Mormon, or whatever). As a parent, the best reaction is to remain consistent in *your* faith while your teen experiments with his. Just because he makes a decision one week does not mean the decision is a permanent one (as a matter of fact, spontaneous decisions usually end up with spontaneous retractions very soon afterward). Experimentation is part of adolescence and part of finding a personal identity, and it is a rare teen that does not stretch the limits at least once a year to see what reactions he can create.

Teens have a strong pull towards the Aspect of Focus—receiving guidance. In gradeschool a simple list of rules was sufficient, now they require that these rules and guidelines make sense. Later in this book you will find resources to help teens understand Judaism's expectations. They are invaluable aids to parents trying to show their teen a spiritual path with a sense of order and consistency. Far from being a lost cause, the teen years abound in opportunities for becoming a truly spiritual person.

And how best to create this desire in a teen? By providing leadership through example. Teens, as we know, are exasperating because they seem to ignore most of what we say.

But the example we provide by our actions cannot be so easily
dismissed, and is perhaps the greatest way of showing our teens
the importance Judaism can play in their lives.

How To Parent A Teen

Parents always wonder how to increase the impact they
have on their teens, and so by popular request, here is a list of
five "Don'ts" directly from the mouths of teens. In character, the
teens insisted that these be negatively worded—they got a kick
out of wagging an imaginary finger at their parents, for a change.
In no particular order, these cardinal errors are almost
guaranteed to make a teen stop listening:

- Don't yell. As one bright child said "We learn by example,
  and what I learned is how to yell back at my dad." (On the
  flip side, many teens said that speaking quietly had a major
  impact.)

- Don't patronize. Talking down to them (including using
  "teen talk") makes them angry.

- Don't generalize. When teens hear the words "you never..."
  or "you always..." , they stop listening. They immediately
  begin thinking of exceptions, instead of listening to what you
  have to say.

- Don't misquote them. Teens feel misunderstood if you "twist
  their words". Better not to quote them at all.

- Don't nag. How many reminders counts as nagging varies
  from child to child. Better to write a reminder note and go
  about your business.

Each age group has its own particular challenges and

opportunities, but they all share the need for leadership. By using ourselves as examples we create the best opening for religious discussions and create in our children a hunger for more. When we as parents, grandparents, and caregivers desire more knowledge, more comfort, more connection or more guidance, we find these appetites echoed in our children. Our children cannot help but follow if we grow our own faith; by being true to our own center, we allow our children to discover theirs.

ଔ   ଔ   ଔ   ଔ   ଔ

Profiling Your Child's Faith

No one has yet fully realized the wealth of sympathy, kindness and generosity hidden in the soul of a child. The effort of every true education should be to unlock that treasure. (Emma Goldman)

෫   ෫   ෫   ෫   ෫

Any parent of two children knows that brothers and sisters are usually very different from each other. It's usually about the time the second child is six months old that one parent remarks to the other "I can't believe that these two children have the same genes! They're like night and day!" A wonderful miracle occurs with each and every child, and part of that miracle is that each child has a unique set of characteristics that makes him perfectly suited for his life tasks. It's a parent's task to coax the finest performance out of each child.

A family rarely has children with the same interests; researchers call this phenomenon "niche picking". The oldest gravitates to a particular area of interest (his 'niche'), the second child chooses a different path, and the following children find their own areas. You see this with faith as well; children within a family normally gravitate towards different faith benefits.

Because each child is unique, developing your child's spirituality takes some thoughtful planning. We have discussed the Four Factors of spirituality—Facts, Feelings, Friends, and Focus, and described which area appeals to each age group. But guidelines based on your child's age alone are general: they are effective only two thirds of the time. To complete the other third, we need to look at personality and interests.

Based on your child's temperament, preferred activities, and your own lifestyle as parents, you can find the best focus for each of your children. Remember, though, that a complete faith requires exposure to *all four* of the faith factors. Just as a house of worship can't be built with just one wall, a child needs all four factors to create a strong link to Judaism. Your child's faith profile will show you where to begin building his or her faith, but *do* expose your child to all the faith benefits of Fact, Feeling, Friends and Focus. As we have seen, people tend to change their primary factor as they mature. Show your child early on that there are many benefits to faith, and they will remain connected to Judaism regardless of where life may take them.

The chart at the end of this chapter will help you put these pieces of information together, developing a Benefit Profile tailored for your child. Then you will be ready to use Part Two—specific examples for each age group. Armed with your child's personal profile and the specifics of his age-group, you will now have a set of personalized guidelines. This blueprint has been tested and are known to work over 95% of the time. But that still leaves children who may fall between categories. If you feel that you know what is appropriate for your child, *follow your instincts!* The best parenting is done from the heart (not the brain), so let your parenting instincts guide your steps.

Profiling your Child

Children are poor men's riches. (English Proverb)

ℭℨ   ℭℨ   ℭℨ   ℭℨ   ℭℨ

You will need to examine three parts of your child's life to come up with a clear picture of the benefit most compelling to her. Her preferred activities (what she most enjoys doing), her temperament (how she copes with daily situations), and her family environment (most specifically, you!) are important pieces of the benefits puzzle. Although *temperament* is the best indicator of their preferences in the long-term, their *activities* and their current *family environment* show how best to catch their attention immediately.

Tanya and Mark provide a good example of how family environment influences faith factors. They are the parents of two young boys, aged eight and eleven, and are two of the warmest, calmest individuals you could ever hope to meet. Their children, although extremely polite and well-mannered, are not what you would consider quiet *or* calm. In fact, they are downright rambunctious. Even though they are normally seen *running* from place to place (they never walk anywhere), they have no problem sitting through a Shabbat service. Their parents have instilled in them a sense of the importance of Shabbat, and the boys are able to set aside their personal preference for activity and spend some quiet time in worship. Mark and Tanya's expectations have influenced how their sons experience their faith.

Children can change dramatically from year to year. Just as your child's preferences for activities will change, his preference for a particular faith benefit may shift as well. Look for ways to **cover each area** at some point in their formative years, and plan on re-evaluating your child's preferences at least every two years. We can't know what our children will come across as adults, and we do well to prepare them for all situations. The more benefits of faith a child sees when he is growing up, the greater the chances that he will stay with that faith as an adult.

Activities

Activity Level: Parents can find what will appeal most to a child by taking a look at her daily activities. Your first clue is physical activity level—how much energy she uses in an average day. Children with high activity levels who seem to be boundless bundles of enthusiasm need movement and physicality. Always looking for physical gratification or a sense of purpose, these children look instinctively for relationships—Friends. They enjoy being with people and will expend considerable energy to be with them. Often, these children are also drawn to Focus, as they value its sense of purpose.

Children who are less *physically* active than their peers probably have more activity occurring on the *inside*. They are more attuned to their internal state than to others, and often seek solitude instead of interaction. These children will most likely gravitate towards Facts or Feelings, depending on their other interests and personal characteristics. Those who are neither high nor low but...well...average, seem to gravitate towards Friends; socializing is a common denominator among children.

Often two children in the same family have dramatically different activity levels. In one family, a hyperactive son is complemented by a daughter who writes poetry and loves to sit by the fireplace and find patterns in the flames. While it has been a challenge for the parents to find activities that they both enjoy, they have found that alternating Friend-focused activities with Feeling endeavors is a way to hold the attention of both their children. Each family presents its own challenges, and you will often need to be creative to find a balance that works.

Preferred Activities: Another important issue to address is the type of activity your child enjoys. Older children are very predictable in their choice of activities; younger children are less definite about their likes and dislikes. (But not always. I remember when my daughter was three, I was determined that she would play with both "boy toys" and "girl toys". I proudly bought her a metal tanker truck and gave it to her with great excitement. She took one look at it and went back to dressing her dolls; the truck was never touched. So much for "gender neutral" parenting.)

Children who prefer books and learning are on a search for understanding, and the area of Facts is where they are most comfortable. This group is relatively uninterested in sports; they prefer their stimulation in the mental sphere instead of the physical. This group normally has fewer close friends than other children, preferring time alone to times with others.

Children who are most interested in quieter pursuits will likely search for emotional content in faith (the Feelings area). These children often read and listen to music, and their inward focus results in few or no close friends. They generally seek support, confirmation and comfort from their parents, more so than the other types. Their sports preferences tend more towards individual sports such as swimming or biking.

On the other hand, some children seem to always be with some of their many friends. Their activities normally occur outside as this group tends to be noisy; they're too loud and physically active to be inside for very long! They normally prefer active team sports, for example soccer and other ball games. These children will have a natural tendency for the Friends aspect of faith.

Lastly, some children form a few very close friendships, and prefer non-competitive sports. They desire to make their friends happy as well as themselves, and dislike the pressure that competition creates. This group seeks guidance as their main benefit (spiritual Focus), looking for rules that govern their actions.

Games: The types of games children enjoy are incredibly diverse. Walk down the games aisle of any large toy store, and you will see every imaginable topic turned into a board or video game, an outside game, a card game, a coloring book *and* a costume. As with the other types of activities, the types of games that children prefer will give you an indication of which faith benefit they will be most interested in.

Children who prefer board games involving strategy, books or word games are clearly involved with thinking. These children are most likely to be focused on the faith benefit of Facts. Those who like group games, quiet play and coloring books are turned inward, and probably tend towards Feelings. Children who prefer to make up their own games and often end up playing alone have an interest in problem-solving, and Focus is probably their preferred pathway to spirituality. Lastly, those who enjoy outside activities and group games will be drawn to the Friends factor.

Personality

> *Children need models rather than critics.*
> *(Joseph Joubert)*

ᘔ   ᘔ   ᘔ   ᘔ   ᘔ

While a child's current activities tell us much about their current interests, personality tells what to expect in the long term. There are many ways to measure personality and temperament in children, but one system that is helpful to us comes from a theory developed by David Kiersey & Marilyn Bates and used in the Kiersey Temperament Sorter[7]. This system describes four distinct personality types that are helpful in understanding a child's spiritual focus.

The first type, who we will call the "Knowledge Seekers", have a pressing desire to understand or explain their world. Known also as the NT, or iNtuitive Thinking personality, children of this personality type are constantly questioning—they are sometimes accused of creating questions they KNOW don't have answers! This personality type enjoys books and usually lists reading as their preferred activity. Children with this temperament style may lack social skills—they prefer the world of ideas to the world of people. Often these youngsters are high achievers academically, and are frequently independent. One NT teenager I know would much rather send email messages to ten people than sit and talk to one person for ten minutes. Such is the world of the NT—often they would rather *think* about something than go out and do it. They are generally unimpressed with participation in family rituals—they don't see the reason! These individuals are drawn by personality to the **Facts** of faith—they look for answers and can be drawn to find them in spirituality.

The Integrity Seekers, also known as the NF personality style (for iNtuitive Feeling), have a pressing need to please others. They are hypersensitive, both to criticism and to the needs of others, and will often go out of their way to right a wrong or ease a hurt. These children generally have excellent language skills and tend to be highly verbal and prolific writers—diaries and poetry writing are the lifeblood of this type. The poetry-writing fire-gazing young lady mentioned earlier is certainly in this category. Integrity Seekers tend to excel in social situations, both because of their language skills and their sensitivity to others. On the negative side, they are prone to daydreaming and fanaticizing. Not surprisingly, these children gravitate towards **Feelings**.

On the complete opposite end of the spectrum are the

Responsibility Seekers, the SJ (*Sensing Judging*) temperament style. These children look for consistency and order in their world, and daydreaming is simply not allowed. They are interested in being productive and completing tasks assigned to them; in school, memory exercises and workbooks bring them great pleasure. Approval from adults is more important to this group than any other; they will often persist in a task until it meets the approval of a parent or teacher. This group truly enjoys the ritual of holiday gatherings and traditions that create a sense of order in their lives. SJ's would not *dream* of messing with a holiday tradition; one child insists that the Hanukkiah be placed in exactly the same spot on the mantle each year. To these individuals, a sense of **Focus** is mandatory. They look for the order and sense of the world, and can find it in spirituality.

The group most often accused of being happy-go-lucky are the "Freedom Seekers" or SP's (*Sensing Perceiving* types). This group is marked by its high activity level and rather impulsive behavior. One parent of two children, one of whom is an SP, complains that her SP son never wants to wait for his SJ sister—she's always too slow for his needs. A Freedom Seeker will change directions at the drop of a hat, often to the frustration of parents and friends. This temperament style is also the messiest of the four types; don't expect a clean room from this one! Children of this temperament enjoy being team members, and are usually more interested in school *activities* than school *learning*. The faith benefit of **Friends** appeals to this type, as their desire for activity and open-ended adventure usually requires an accomplice.

Environment & Family

> *One of the most obvious facts about grown ups to a child is that they have forgotten what it is like to be a child. (Randall Jarrell)*

48

Temperament and activities are both issues that are internal to your child. However, children are influenced by many external forces as well. In fact, perhaps the most critical influence of all comes from you—the family. This fact should not be surprising since many of your child's waking hours are spent under the watchful eye of a parent or caretaker. Even when playing down the street with friends, most children know what their parents expect of them (Now, whether they *do* these things is another story, and another book….)

Likewise, children also know their parents' preferences about how faith should be practiced. How do they know? If the parents attend Bible study groups each week, children learn the importance of study. If parents spend time after services with friends from the congregation, or make a point of getting together with other "religious" friends, children see the close friendships created. Parents who discuss God's love and care, and comment on how good they feel after services, communicate those feelings to their children. And if children see their parents asking the rabbi or minister for guidance, they understand the importance of being directed by their faith.

You, in turn, have created these "family norms" because of outside factors. Perhaps your parents always celebrated Hanukkah in a particular way, or maybe your congregation provides a potluck oneg after services, and so these traditions become your own. In this manner, spiritual practices cross generations, giving us traditions that bring the comfort of familiarity.

The influence of family is always greater in younger children. They have less choice about their own activities, and are normally quite happy to follow along with family traditions. Older children and teens are less likely to do something just because the family wants them to do it. But that shouldn't stop you from inviting them! Whatever they grow up with becomes more comfortable in adulthood; most adults prefer familiar territory.

The impact of family traditions can vary from child to child based on culture and family history. Some cultures, such as Asian and South American traditions, place a high value on family ties. These bonds can cross over into faith, creating a strong connection between a child and his family's faith tradition. Temperament plays a part here as well; independent children are less likely to carry on family traditions 100%, preferring to cut their own paths. But even when family traditions are left behind, the family influence continues to make itself felt in other, less visible ways.

Adults often retain strong memories from childhood that seem to permeate the manner in which they raise their own children. One mother of an infant said her strongest Jewish memory was of her Bubbe's food. She can still remember the smells wafting out to greet her when she came in from playing, giving her a sense of Jewish culture. Her husband has different memories that shape his feelings about Judaism today. He remembers being given a strong sense of his heritage as a young boy, and today looks at his faith as a way of life. Because of the values he grew up with, Judaism has become a natural part of his identity. While this couple may not continue any specific traditions from their own families, they clearly made a commitment to Judaism based on memories of Jewish households.

ଓ   ଓ   ଓ   ଓ   ଓ

How To Use The Benefit Profiler

Below is a chart that summarizes all of these areas—activities, temperament, and environment. The chart includes spaces for three children, or for one child at three different ages. Use the chart to decide the most important faith benefit for him or her, which will direct you to the most relevant chapters in Part Two. You may come up with *two* areas that tie for first place. You can either use what you know about your child to break the tie, or pursue both areas equally. For your convenience each area is briefly summarized below. When you decide which description best fits your child put an "X" on the correct line. Then simply count up the X's in each column, and you have your profile!

CHILD/TIME #1

AREA	Facts	Feelings	Friends	Focus
Developmental Group				
Activity Level				
Activity Type				
Preferred Games				
Temperament				
Family Focus				
TOTAL				

CHILD/TIME #2

AREA	Facts	Feelings	Friends	Focus
Developmental Group				
Activity Level				
Activity Type				
Preferred Games				
Temperament				
Family Focus				
TOTAL				

Developmental Group
If your child is in: Put an "X" in:

Preschool   Friends
Elementary   Facts and Friends
Middle School   Facts or Feelings (choose)
High School/Teens   Focus, and
                                 Facts or Feelings (choose)

Activity Level
If your child'a activity level is: Put an "X" in:

Low (high internal)   Facts and Feelings
High (low internal)   Friends and Focus

Activity Type
If your child enjoys: Put an "X" in:

Books & study, quite times, few sports   Facts
Non-competitive sports, few close friends   Feelings
Outside activities, team sports   Friends
Individual sports, quiet activities,
few friends   Focus

Preferred Games
And if they also like: Put an "X" in:
Strategy & word games   Facts
Coloring books, quiet games   Feelings
Made up games, solitary play   Focus
Outside, group games   Friends

Temperament (Mark two "X's" if your child is extremely similar to the description in the text.)

If your child is a:	Put an "X" in:
Knowledge-Seeker	Facts
Integrity-Seeker	Feelings
Responsibility-Seeker	Focus
Freedom-Seeker	Friends

Family Focus (You may use two X's if your family emphasizes two different activities)

If your family:	Put an "X" in:
Attends study groups & workshops	Facts
Stresses love of God, good feelings	Feelings
Goes to social activities with congregation members	Friends
Encourages prayers for guidance	Focus

53

5
Different Paths, Different Choices

We must never cease to question our own faith and ask what God means to us. (Abraham Joshua Heschel)

ભ   ભ   ભ   ભ   ભ

To help each child find their unique spiritual path, we need to understand the unique and special nature of the four aspects of faith. Each of the aspects creates a unique path to faith, forging a particular course towards the same ultimate goal. If we think of a pyramid, a four-sided shape reaching to the sky, we see how the four aspects support each other. When we are at the bottom of the pyramid looking up, all we can see is one side of the structure. But as we climb one face to reach the top, the other sides move closer to us. When we reach the top, we discover that all four sides converge, and all paths have been directed towards the same goal. Just so, our climb to God through faith ultimately leads to the same destination as the paths that others choose. And if we change paths along the way and choose another course (another aspect of faith), the eventual destination remains the same.

Creating an early connection to faith is important, for ties formed in childhood become life-long bonds. Despite the bends in the road along the journey of life, a solid bond to Judaism creates a connection to past and future generations. This extension through time is part of the Jewish commission to heal the world—to create a community of spiritual beings committed to the betterment of all. By setting your child on this path, you play an important part in God's plan for the world.

It is important to introduce children to each of the four aspects of faith so that when the events of life move them to another face on the pyramid they will recognize the territory. Nearly everyone experiences a shift in priorities at some point in life; jobs and families almost guarantee that what we consider essential today will be lower on our list at some future time. We can prepare our children in advance for these changes by showing them *all* of the benefits of faith. Even though they seem firmly entrenched in the Friends aspect now, we can introduce them to Focus so they can make use of it later. When the world seems to shift before their eyes (as when they get an apartment, go to college, or get married) the familiar territory of Judaism and faith can become a great sense of comfort.

Each aspect contains several "hooks" that will draw your child into spirituality; the descriptions here give you general guidelines on the types of resources that children will find useful. Use the ideas presented here as a springboard to create activities that are unique to your child and your family; later in the book you will find a complete resource list with further suggestions.

"Just the Facts, Ma'am": The Path of Intellect

Children who are drawn to **Facts** demand a reason for everything. "Why is it called the Bible?" "Why does God care what we do?" "Why do we stand up when we pray?" and on, seemingly forever. These questions, although a mere annoyance to parents, are actually essential activities for fact-focused children and young people. Their world is categorized into "what makes sense" and "what doesn't". Anything in the no-sense pile is likely to be ignored.

If your child constantly questions everything, it is best to find answers to those queries. Adults most often leave their faith because religion doesn't make sense to them: they never received answers to those important "Why" questions. Consequently they decided that religion could not create order in their world, and went looking for another system that made more sense.

Fortunately, parents don't need to know all the answers to keep their children involved in Judaism. Books are the lifeblood of this group, and they love to be directed to these resources. A note of caution: don't fall into the trap of answering your son with "I don't know, go look it up!" Make it a point to know which book or source is likely to hold the answer to his question. Take the time to sit on his bed and look for the information together. Remember, *your example is the best teacher.* Even if you have absolutely no interest in knowing the answer, be sure that he knows you want *him* to understand.

For this group, the best resources are books. Children that are 100% "fact" oriented will not be impressed by all of your efforts to make up games and special activities—they'd rather just read it and be done with it! Younger children (pre-readers) can find puzzles and museum visits interesting, but only if they include new information.

History: For some children, especially middle-school students who are just learning world history, the past can be fascinating. The study of religious history is an excellent way to learn the meaning of things. History can provide the background for understanding religious rituals, the religious calendar, holiday observances, and many other areas. To younger children, simply knowing the facts of religious history can be exciting. Games that award points for correct answers (Bible trivia and other games) can be fun as well.

Because history is loaded with facts and information, it is a natural beginning for Fact-oriented children. Remember that when children ask difficult questions, history may hold the answers. If your daughter asks the meaning of a particular ritual, it's easy to go to a history book and find the first mention of it. Even if you can't find the complete answer, you will have shown her that her questions are important.

Scripture Study: The answer to many "why" questions comes from the primary source—scripture itself. For the curious child, scripture is more than just a listing of rules to follow; it can open the door to truly understanding the foundations of faith.

But even for older children, the language of scripture can be off-putting. When a child has to struggle just to understand *what* is being said, the *why* may never be reached. Be sure to have a commentary or summary of scripture in "real English"— something your children can understand easily. Children approaching bar/bat mitzvah should have access to a Bible commentary series; the combination of history and classic interpretation brings added depth that Fact-oriented children will appreciate. Commentaries also serve as an extra copy of Torah, as they contain the biblical text as well as the thoughts and ideas of historical scholars.

Talmud is an excellent scriptural reference for older children. Its organization as logical arguments can be extremely exciting to Fact-oriented minds. Not only does the Talmud contain Jewish law, it also holds a wealth of narrative, theology, and ethics. It can open a new world of Judaism to the curious, creating a life-long link between faith and intellect.

Understanding Rituals & Holidays: The purposes for many religious practices often become fuzzy to us as adults; we just do the rituals "because we should". Fact-oriented children need reasons for their actions. Children with this real need-to-know often feel proud of their knowledge, and will use it to excel in their religious school classrooms. When Fact-oriented children don't have access to answers they often are uncomfortable in class, feeling foolish that they can't answer the teacher's questions.

There are many resources *describing* rituals and holiday practices; children using the aspect Fact need *understanding* as well. Be sure that the resources you choose provide answers to these important questions.

Internet Resources: The internet usually attracts Fact-oriented children like bees to honey. Their natural tendency to devour information is fed by the internet's inexhaustible web of references and facts. There are hundreds of sites out there, but not all contain factual information. Jewish and child-oriented "webrings" are becoming more prevalent, where sites with similar content are linked in a ring format (meaning you can always circle the ring in cyberspace and return to your starting point). These sites are also evaluated for appropriate content, so you are assured that your child will not electronically surf into shark-infested waters. Yahoo! (www.yahoo.com) is a good way to find sites; their reviews and site descriptions provide helpful information. Once you have found fun and interesting sites, bookmark the pages and let them surf on!

Information And Word Games: Fact-oriented children love words and facts. Encyclopedias that would never be touched by other children hold a special fascination for these young detectives. (I know one budding scientist who puts a reference book next to her bed at night, "just in case" she dreams about something she can't answer!) There should be a reference book in every home that has Fact-oriented children; these are books they are likely to take with them when they leave home.

Trivia games are also exciting to children with a Fact orientation. The challenge of telling someone what you know *and* beating your sister or friend at the same time is an irresistible combination. These games should be high on your the list if you have a fact-focused child.

Once more with Feeling: On the Path of Emotion

For a certain group of children, faith is most important in its ability to create positive feelings. The children in this group are drawn to the peace and comfort they feel after listening to music or attending services. Children for whom **Feelings** are important often gravitate towards music and prayer as the most rewarding elements of their faith. These are the children who are most often found in services with their parents; they seem to be drawn to the softer side of religion and truly enjoy the feelings of peace that spirituality brings.

Many adults can remember times when they were concerned by the death of a grandparent, or had a close call in an auto accident. In these times, we were able to turn to God for a sense of peace regardless of the outcome. Even if Gramps died after all, we felt taken care of in important ways and this sense of safety stayed with us as a long-lasting memory of the positive side of faith. Children who are primarily attracted to the Feelings aspect often seek these same assurances, asking God to make things right.

While not a large group, those searching for Feelings have very specific ways in which they are touched by faith. If they do not feel connected emotionally it is unlikely that they will remain interested in Judaism, as the need for emotional contact is very important to this group. For very young children, the most important emotion is probably joy—having *fun* with religion! They will remember these good times later, and turn to spirituality when they need comfort. Regardless of the primary faith benefit children seek, they all need to see faith as a warm, inviting part of life. As the inevitable traumas of life appear, faith provides a safe haven and a shelter from life's trials.

Prayer Resources: For adults, prayer is one of the primary ways in which religious feelings are explored. Reciting group prayers, for example, often brings a sense of peace. In children, too, prayer is an important element in their spiritual life. The concept of prayer is easily introduced by teaching children standard prayers that they can say every day. Youngsters who are drawn to the feeling side of faith will be very interested in the idea of "sitting quietly and thinking about God," an introduction to meditative prayer. There are many ways to encourage your child in regular prayer; for younger children, set aside a time each day to recite simple blessings. Older ones are best left to find their own prayer times, just be sure to allow them the privacy they need.

Religious Services: After personal prayer, religious services are second in popularity with those people seeking the aspect of feelings. For this group, weekly services create an inner peace, often emerging from the liturgical music and prayers. Children under ten years old cannot explain *why* they enjoy services, but those focused on feeling will generally be very happy to join their parents in worship. Preteen and teenage girls may gravitate towards this aspect of faith for a time as they start to explore the emotional part of themselves. Many congregations offer children's services that work well for younger children, although these events are certainly not quiet, meditative experiences (but they generally *are* fun).

Music Resources: Yet another powerful source of religious feelings, music has the ability to touch our souls like nothing else. From wordless melodies to familiar tunes, children drawn to the emotional side of faith enjoy being surrounded by song. Music can be listened to, sung or played; give your children opportunities for all three. Many Feeling-oriented children also play an instrument, so sheet music to some familiar Jewish tunes is a great addition to their music library. From an early age, children will enjoy singing in a choir. If your congregation has a children's choir encourage them to join. At home, the simple act of playing religious music can create a positive association for these children.

Home Traditions: "Feeling" children appreciate the comfort of familiar rituals and holiday traditions. Holidays spent with family, whether it includes uncles and grandparents or just mom and dad, have an important place in the hearts of these youngsters. The warm feelings and fun associated with holiday meals, gift-giving, and song creates a powerful sense of connection with their spiritual roots. Think back to your own memories of childhood—it's likely that the clearest recollections are related to holidays. Rituals that remain constant from year to year are very important for these children. The rituals can be as simple as lighting candles or as complex as a complete Passover *seder*—it's the constancy that matters, not the substance.

When Friendship Counts Most: Charting the Path to Relationship

Children, like their parents, are social creatures. Many children are naturally drawn to the factor of relationship (or **Friends**) through their normal desire to be part of a group. In fact, many rabbis would say (as mine used to) that to truly practice Judaism, one must do it with others. The goal of this aspect isn't simply to *be with* others, it is to *connect to* others, to create a common bond. In children, this connection starts simply by being with other Jewish children. As friendships begin to form, the shared experience of Judaism creates a closer connection to each other and to the Jewish faith.

One teen, reflecting on his younger days ("when I was a kid", as he said,) mentioned vivid recollections of lighting a *hanukkiah* at a friend's house one evening. "I wasn't at home when it came time to light the candles, so my friend's mom invited me to stay. Being with my friend made it more special for me—it was something we could share."

There are many ways to bring connections and relationship into your child's Jewish experiences. With the introduction of the internet, some of these connections can be "virtual" as well. But whether in real or electronic time, connections are vital to the child who has the Factor of Friends as his or her first choice. In younger children, simple exposure to other Jewish families is a great beginning. From middle school on, however, the opportunity to make true friendships with other Jewish youth is critical in creating a lasting tie to Judaism. Fortunately, there are many avenues available to meet those needs.

Pen Pals: Although it's an old fashioned concept, regular correspondence with other Jews is one important way to build connections to the world's Jewish community. One modernization comes from the introduction of the internet—"virtual" penpals are now available to those with an internet connection. But whether real or virtual, connecting with others around the globe is a powerful way to feel connections within the Jewish community that exist across oceans and continents. For younger children, stories of contemporary Jews in other lands accomplishes the same goal. Many children will need a push to continue the correspondence, but the connections they make can serve them well later. Stories abound of friends who kept up their pen-and-ink correspondence for several years; one 40-year-old woman tells of a Jewish friend in Japan. What an eye-opener to discover the difference in Passover and Hanukkah rituals in Asian countries!

Contemporary Stories: Children looking to "connect" with other Jews can relate well to stories of their peers. In listening to stories of others, they can feel vicariously the trials and triumphs of others similar to themselves. Most of these youngsters do not have much interest in books, so stories longer than an hour's reading time are likely to fall flat. Movies, however, are good ways to bring this idea home. There are many great videos with Jewish themes involving children; renting one of these movies each month makes a great way to keep your child connected to their faith.

Youth Groups: Belonging to a group is extremely important to children, and to these youngsters in particular. Particularly after age ten, identifying oneself as a member of a specific group is important in forming a spiritual identity. It is important to find some group where your Friends-seeking child is comfortable. The group may be merely grouped by age, as a Hebrew school class, or may revolve around a particular activity such as scouting (yes, there are Jewish scout troops.) But being uncomfortable in a group can be a major turn-off; do some investigating until you find a group your child truly feels comfortable with.

Group Holiday Celebrations: Sharing holidays is yet another way to create connection. Celebrations involving other families and children, whether they be a simple Shabbat dinner or a community Passover *seder*, bind children (and adults) to their Jewish community. Jewish celebrations are meant to be either family or community events; be sure to use this idea to the benefit of your children that seek connection. For this group, the more the merrier; bring in as many people as you can comfortable bear. Your children will thank you for it.

Day/Summer Camps: While long-term projects are good, sometimes a short-term dose of friendship is just what's needed. Many week-long opportunities exist for children to explore their Jewish roots in an "intensive" experience. Some synagogues offer programs during winter break; others provide weekend experiences for children in their school program. And of course, summer camps are available that can span several weeks. If at all possible, children focused on "Friends" should participate in one of these activities each year. Some of these programs can be the same price as daycare, and scholarship programs are common.

Focus on Focus: Choosing the Path of Guidance

Rules guide our lives, and children pursuing the Aspect of Guidance (**Focus**) look to faith to provide the rulebook. Each day children are faced with dozens of decisions to make: "Should I tell my teacher how I really feel?" "I know Sharon cheated on the test. What should I do about it?" "I really want to go to camp, but my parents can't afford it. Should I mention it to them or not?" Faith provides a code of ethical behavior that points the way through the web of possibilities.

Focus-oriented children look for order and consistency in their lives. "If it's Tuesday, it must be fish for dinner", and so on. For these youngsters, Judaism's main appeal is likely to be the way in which it provides guidance for our lives. As one college student put it: "I have learned many things about myself and my religion. I now have more confidence and guidance to help me in present and future times."

These children need ways to combine Judaism with daily life. Making their faith a normal part of daily activities is the best way to provide a solid background to those boys and girls looking for Focus. Almost any activity can bring Judaism into the picture, from setting the table (with Judaica placemats) to doing homework (with a Star of David pencil).

For this group, perhaps more than for any other, parents and caregivers play an essential part in linking their child to Judaism. Your example is the best "hook" to bring children closer to their faith; being a model of what you expect from them is critical in showing them the value of Judaism. When children grow up with Judaism as a regular part of their day, they naturally turn to their faith later in life to answer deeper ethical dilemmas. Important resources here include knowing Jewish ethical guidelines and incorporating Judaic customs into daily practices.

Heroes And Role Models: Children who gravitate towards Focus need real examples of Judaism in action. The more ways they can see Jewish principles applied, the stronger their ties will be with their spiritual heritage. Both traditional biblical figures and modern-day examples are important here; make sure some characters are the same age as your child, and you will create a package that will give your child strong and long-lasting reasons to be involved in their faith.

One role model story will be familiar to many adults— the lesson of Sandy Kofax. His strong statement in refusing to pitch in the World Series on *Yom Kippur* was a lesson in strength to many young men in the 1960s. Said one father of two in an interview, "Sandy Kofax made me proud to be Jewish. He stood up for what he believed in, and I realized that being Jewish was something really important." I wish for *your* children role models like that.

Values: Learning the relationship between values and faith is important for all children. "Focus-seekers" have a natural inclination to find the correct process for any task, and so learning values comes easily to this group. Teaching by example is, of course, the best way to show values to children—an action is worth a thousand words. There are also many Jewish fables and folk tales that demonstrate values; Jews have been teaching by story-telling for hundreds of years.

Ritual Practices: Yet another way to keep a child in touch with his or her faith is to become aware of Jewish ritual practices. Judaism is full of different ways to give thanks to God and celebrate events; your Focus-oriented child will find these prayers and rituals important. The best way to show your child ritual practices is to join him or her. How special a child feels when helping to light the Shabbat candles and say the blessings together!

Craft Projects: Closely tied to ritual practices are ritual objects, and constructing one from scratch makes it even more special. Creating a family menorah, *tzedakah* box, or *challah* cover can be particularly rewarding when the object is used regularly. Making every-day objects with a Jewish touch (how about bookmarks with a Jewish star?) is yet another way to bring Judaism into daily life. The options are almost limitless; an active imagination is the best resource possible.

Home Judaica: An important and natural way to foster spirituality in your child is to make it a natural part of their surroundings. Children who can see their ties to Judaism displayed in every room come to see it as a natural part of life. In fact, they may be extremely bothered if it is NOT visible; I've known parents who had to ship a favorite picture across country to comfort their college-age children. Every room in the house can have something Jewish included; these articles become valued possessions to be passed on through generations.

The Next Step

We have seen the varied paths that lead to a stronger link to Judaism. It should be clear by now that something that is a major turn-on to one child may be a royal turn-*off* to another. Whatever the age of your child (or children), NOW is the time to begin. Preschoolers are great investigators—give them something Jewish as a focus for their activities. School-age children love new tasks; spirituality is a great focus for their new skills. Teens and preteens will benefit just as much from these efforts as younger children; it is never too late to show a child the value of spirituality. A strong foundation in faith is built day by day based on a commitment to long-term involvement in

Judaism and the Jewish community. The sooner the task is begun, the stronger your child's bonds to faith will become.

We have looked at some general guidelines for guiding your children to Judaism, but there are specific issues that need to be dealt with as well. How do you introduce your child to Torah? How do you teach about God? And what about values— how do you start? The next chapters will give you a map for these thorny roadways. Using what you now know about the four paths to faith, you can begin to serve as a guide for your child's journey to Judaism.

ଓ   ଓ   ଓ   ଓ   ଓ

6
Teaching Values, Teaching Torah

The ultimate goal is to transform the world into the kind of world God had in mind when He created it. (Harold Kushner)

ભ   ભ   ભ   ભ   ભ

Some parts of life are too critical to be left to chance; teaching values to our children is one such issue. Values and ethics tell us what we stand for as Jews and how we can deal with life's challenges, and make Judaism an essential touchstone in our lives. Our task as parents and grandparents is to instill these ideals in the next generation of Jews. It is our mission to make the children in our charge even better than we are ourselves, bringing the world closer to the place God intended it to be. Each of us is uniquely fashioned to do just that: the rabbis taught that each of us is uniquely created to fill our place in the world (and in our families). Had there ever been a person exactly like us, there would be no need for us to have been born.

There is a story in Genesis about a man who seals Joseph's fate. Joseph's father asks him to check after his brothers, but they are no where to be found. An unknown man appears, directs Joseph to his brothers, and disappears again. We

aren't told the man's name, he is simply *ish*, a man. Had this man
not been there, or not been willing to assist a wayward traveler,
history would have been very different. Joseph would not have
been sold by his brothers, the Hebrew nation would never have
become slaves in Egypt, and there might never have been the need
for Moses to part the Red Sea and receive the Ten
Commandments. Just like the unknown *ish*, each of is a critical
thread in the tapestry of life, and in the lives of our family
members. We can never know exactly what place we or our
children hold in history, for we cannot step back and look at the
entire emerging piece of art. But we can be ready to take our part
when the time comes; the first step is to practice and teach the
values of our faith.

Our values, of course, come from Torah. One cannot
study Torah without learning values, for we see living examples
of values in the weekly Torah and Haftarah segments. Children
need actual examples to understand concepts such as *ḥesed* and
tzedakah; these abstract ideas take shape only after they read
them in Torah and connect them to daily life. Parents often ask
how to begin studying Torah with their children. The best way is
to tie Torah study into events in daily life, creating a natural
bridge between the study of God's word and understanding how
God wants us to act.

When you use Torah to teach values, you have the
pleasure of beginning your child's Jewish education at home in a
simple and straightforward fashion. When parents think of
"teaching Torah", they often imagine hours of intense study over
obscure passages of text. It needn't be that way; torah study can
be as simple as telling stories.

If there is a perfect way to study values and Torah, it
might be this: you notice 10-year-old Jeremy treating your
elderly neighbor with kindness, offering to help bring his
groceries indoors. When Jeremy finishes, you complement him

70

on his actions, and tell him he has just practiced *ḥesed*, or kindness. Later on, perhaps just before bed, you offer to show him another story of *ḥesed* and bring out the book of Ruth. Together you go through the short story of Ruth and discuss the kindness that Ruth shows her mother-in-law and the kindness that Boaz later shows to them both. Of course, this is the ideal. Life being what it is, it might be several days before you label his helpfulness, and even later when you mention the biblical account. Perhaps you will only be able to talk about the story, and not read it together. But regardless of the form, the steps are the same:

1. <u>Comment</u> on his positive actions; catch him being good.

2. <u>Label</u> his action with its Jewish name and mention other examples.

3. <u>Read or tell</u> a story from Torah that gives an example of the value he practiced.

Aside from a *Tanach* (bible) or an anthology of children's Bible stories, the only preparation you need for this type of Torah teaching is a watchful eye to notice your child's acts of kindness. The rabbis teach that there are many levels of studying Torah, and by taking this approach you are working on two levels— description and interpretation. First, you are describing the story, providing facts and details. You are also interpreting the story, explaining the lesson behind the details. Not only are you teaching Jewish history, you are also showing that there is more than a surface story; that God put the Torah together in a fashion that carries lessons from age to age.

Perhaps the best section of Torah for the study of values is the *parshah Kedoshim*, found in Leviticus chapter 19. Known as the "holiness code", it was given to Moses by God to be proclaimed "to the entire assembly of the Children of Israel". The rabbis took this to mean that each Jew is required to work towards these ideals; no one is excluded from seeking holiness. The values described here describe the ways we are to treat others — honoring our parents, avoiding gossip, not seeking revenge, etc. This passage provides an excellent place to start when preteens and teens ask "so what does being a good Jew mean, anyway?" In a nutshell, the holiness code describes God's expectations for his people, the Jews. The Jewish perspective is that all people begin as "pure", meaning without sin. But God asks more of us. Not only are we to be without sin, but we are to take the next step to strive for holiness and to exercise restraint even in those things that God has permitted.

Children can't keep a catalog of shoulds and shouldn'ts in memory. Even as adults, we seldom ask ourselves "now, what's the Jewish value that I can apply here?" As with spirituality, our goal is to internalize these values, making them an "of course!", something we can't *not* do. We help our children accomplish this task by encouraging them to treat others as they wish to be treated. Even if your daughter doesn't remember the name of the value she is practicing, you label it for her later and congratulate her on being a mensch.

When we live by our values, we create an automatic return; we feel positive, the recipient is enriched, and we often receive a measure of the same value in return. Honesty is a perfect example. When we practice honesty in our relationships, those whose hearts we touch automatically return honesty to us. Such is the nature of values.

Using the Aspects in Teaching Values

We need to use ways that speak to our children personally when we teach them values. Each child's faith factor, the main "hook" that draws him or her to spirituality, requires a different path to create a values-oriented adult. Children applying the aspect of **Facts** need an understanding of the full meaning and intention of each value. More than just learning a definition, intellectually-oriented children want to know why the value is important. Older children and teens with this orientation enjoy creating hypothetical worlds where a certain value does not exist: what would happen, for example, if it was OK to lie?

Children that have a primary emphasis on **Feelings** will be most receptive to the positive emotions that result from engaging in these actions. The Hebrew expression *simcha shel mitzvah* (joy of good deeds) refers to the satisfaction that comes from acting with virtue. For this group of children, this emotional response is important. Children in this group also need praise when they use important values; acknowledgement for good deeds makes the link between values and feeling good about oneself much stronger.

The **Friends** factor demands a connection to others, so group efforts at learning and practicing values are important. The contagious nature of practicing values is also a positive hook for this group. Learning and practicing values in a family situation, particularly when parents are involved, is a big attraction for Friends-oriented children.

Of the four factors, perhaps the one that provides the clearest link to learning values is **Focus.** In their search for guidance, children who emphasize this factor naturally seek the rules for living that are provided by values. These children are looking for direction—how things are *supposed* to be done. Reminding them that Jewish values are part of being Jewish can be enough to get them started; they will be attracted by the good feelings and sense of satisfaction that comes from using them. Role models are important; they will watch parents and other caregivers for clues on how to act and react.

Of course, the concepts you can teach will become more difficult as your children grow older. For preschoolers, simply knowing the names of some values and creating a positive emotional connection to "being good" is a wonderful start. Elementary age children can begin to identify examples of these values in their lives and think of ways to practice them (for example, to practice kindness to a teacher). In the middle school years, the most important approach to values is to join a group that actively practices these values such as scouting, congregational youth groups, or a service club. Teens can dig more deeply into the meanings of these values, and often enjoy discussing limits and exceptions to Jewish expectations (when, for example, it is permissible to lie). Of course, all age groups should receive comments and praise for any actions or comments that show they are using the values you have taught them.

There are many values that guide our actions and many Torah stories that illustrate them. Choosing the most important principles for living is clearly somewhat arbitrary; contained here are eight core Jewish values that provide children with a strong foundation in how to act and how to treat others. Some values begin with actions towards others which then effect us, while others begin with us and then affect others. Whichever way the pendulum swings, the intent is not merely to pay lip service to the concept, but to create in our children an internal conviction that these ideals are essential. Teaching values is about creating an "Of course!" that comes from realizing that there is only one possible response. When you see a need, you fill it. No avoiding, no procrastination, no wavering. It is a response that comes naturally from us, and affects everyone around us. These values create a person that is most rightly called a *mensch*—what a human being is meant to be.

> *We must once again be dreamers of a better world, binding our children to us with the intensity of our moral worth, the beauty of our historical and ethical vision. (Anne Roiphe)*

಩   ಩   ಩   ಩   ಩

74

Values guiding behavior towards others

Duty to do good (*mitzvah*): The word *mitzvah* (plural, *mitzvot*) as used in common language means a "good deed". As a value, the concept goes much deeper. To perform a mitzvah is *to do what is expected;* to do the actions that God wanted us to do naturally. In a sense, our willingness to do good deeds is a measure of our distance from God: the greater the reluctance, the greater the distance. For Jews, there are two types of *mitzvot*: those directed towards God and those directed towards others. Many of the 613 *mitzvot* mentioned in the Bible are between us and God. It makes no difference to anyone else, for example, if we say morning prayers. But the sense of peace and connection that arises from performing this act is a personal reward from God, a "Well done!" that makes us return for more.

There are many examples in Torah that can be used in teaching about *mitzvot*. One significant *mitzvah* was performed by Abraham and described in Genesis, chapter 18 (*parshah Vayeira*). Three men appear outside the tent of Abraham and Sarah, and even though they are strangers Abraham welcomes them and prepares a festive meal. The story portrays the *mitzvah* of welcoming the stranger and providing hospitality. Since it occurs immediately after the circumcision of Abraham and his household, it is the first *mitzvah* performed by the Jewish people. This story describes one act of kindness that most children can relate to—inviting guests to your home.

The value of performing mitzvot is easy to teach because of the natural happiness that follows each deed—the *simcha shel mitzvot* mentioned earlier. Deeds we do for others such as giving assistance and sharing our possessions automatically bring this joyful feeling. For children, family *mitzvah* projects are a wonderful introduction to the concept of *mitzvot*. Some ideas for family *mitzvah* projects are:

- Saying daily prayers together as a family
- Volunteering at a senior center
- Giving a party for someone of limited means
- Helping someone learn a new skill

Duty to help justly (*tzedakah*): There is no society without its poor; the duty to provide for those less fortunate is an important value to pass to our children. Children understand generosity, sharing, and the idea that one should give without expecting anything in return. When we provide for the needs of others we acknowledge the bonds between people; as Jews we are told to continue giving until all people can fulfill their own needs.

The great Jewish sage Maimonides provides a helpful guide teach children about giving *tzedakah*. He wrote of seven levels of giving, each more positive than the one preceding it. The first level is to give when asked, but begrudgingly. Second is to give willingly, but only what is asked. Third and fourth levels are to give more than asked, and to give before being asked. The last three levels are to give anonymously, to give without knowing the recipient of your gift, and lastly to give so that another becomes self-sufficient. Once children know the various levels of giving, they can be involved in deciding where and how to give *tzedakah*. It is important to remind them that *every* level of *tzedakah*, even the lowest, is still important and provides help for those in need.

Even young children can understand that some people need extra assistance, and they can help decide who deserves a donation from the family. There are many ways to teach this important value:

- Encourage children to give a small part of their allowance or chore money to a special cause.

76

- Have a tzedakah box or *pushke* in some visible place, and encourage regular donations.
- Make charity a family decision; decide together which group to give a donation to several times a year.

Giving Love (_Hesed_) While giving one's money is to be valued, giving of one's person is even more so. Giving _ḥesed_, or acts of lovingkindness, requires a personal involvement that surpasses offerings from one's pocketbook. For several reasons, _ḥesed_ is considered by many to be a higher form of giving. First of all, the 20% limit on donations from one's income does not apply to giving love; there is no limitation on lovingkindness. Next, giving charity is restricted to the poor; lovingkindness can be provided to all. In Jewish law, burial of the dead is _ḥesed_ par excellence, because it is given without any possible hope of return from the recipient.

An excellent "teaching text" on ḥesed is provided in the book of Ruth. The story of Naomi, Ruth and Boaz shows multiple examples of lovingkindness in action. After Ruth's husband dies, Naomi, her mother-in-law, grows poor and decides to leave her home for a foreign land. Ruth provides the first example of ḥesed by deciding to leave her house as well and go with Naomi so she will not be alone. When they arrive, the landowner Boaz again shows ḥesed to them both by providing food and shelter. The story is short and a wonderfully positive bedtime reading. If you are not familiar with the story, now is a great time to read it for yourself.

The very heart of _ḥesed_ is that it be given freely without any thought of a return. It is the one-way nature of the gift of love that is its greatest value. When children master this unselfish motivation, they understand the true essence of this important value. There are several ways in which parents or grandparents can teach children to give love:

- Point out when people need help, and suggest how they can do it.

- Help them send a note to someone or visit them when they are sick or have suffered a loss.

- Encourage them to think of helping someone before they ask

- Give them hugs and kind words when you see them doing an act of lovingkindness.

Concern for Creation: As stewards of the earth, we are called to be concerned with the welfare of all God's creation. This charge includes care for animals as fellow creatures of God, and concern for nature as it is entrusted to us. We are charged to avoid bringing pain or suffering to animals, and to halt any exploitation of the earth. We are the piece of creation that is in "God's image", and as such we must defend the rest of the planet from harm or destruction. The Hebrew terms *tzaar baalei hayyim* (concern for suffering of all creatures) and *shemirat ha-adamah* (protection of the earth) describes the Jewish attitude towards these duties.

Our task to protect the earth leads naturally to a retelling of the creation story. Genesis chapters 1 and 2 (*parshah B'reshit*) tells the familiar story of God's creation, beginning with earth and sea, and ending with humankind. The story leads naturally to a discussion of how we should treat God's creation, as we are to "master the earth, and rule the fish of the sea, the birds of the sky, and all the living things" (Genesis 1:27). Does mastery mean using the earth as we want, or should we also be concerned with the earth's welfare? If we rule all living creatures, does that mean we can destroy their homes and their chances of survival, or should we also make sure they can continue to multiply and prosper?

There are many ways to practice these values. Animal care societies and environmental groups exist in most cities, and most are extremely grateful for gifts of time or money. It is easy for children to practice these values; caring for a pet or enjoying playtime outside is a first step to becoming aware of our responsibility to maintain God's creation. There are many other ways to instill a love of nature in children:

- Go on a nature walk or hike, taking only pictures and leaving only footsteps.

- Volunteer at a local animal rescue service.

- Take care of a neighbor's pets when they go on a trip.

- Become members of the Sierra Club or other environmental advocacy group.

- Subscribe to an environmental magazine.

- Recycle, and donate unwanted items instead of throwing them out.

Values Guiding our Personal Behavior

The values above begin with our actions towards others and end up affecting us as well. Other values begin with our own behavior and radiate outwards, touching the others with whom we interact. One hallmark of these values is the response of others: people want to return the same to you. Four of these core values are peace (*shalom*), truth (*emet*), good speech (*lashon tov*), and respect (*kaved*). Since these values begin internally, the best way to teach these lessons is to catch your child in the act, and then point out what they have done and why you appreciate it.

Peace (*shalom*): A sense of peace always begins at the individual level and spreads outwards. Feelings of peace are difficult to come by in these times; so many forces work towards disruption that experiencing peacefulness, even for short periods, is truly a goal worth obtaining. Certain individuals, places, and actions automatically give us peaceful feelings; a good first step in teaching your child about *shalom* is to expose them to these people or places that bring peace.

The root for the Hebrew word *shalom* means wholeness. We become "whole" beings when we practice peace, healing arguments by giving up our need to be right. We allow humanity to become whole also, for peace brings individuals closer together. The story of Jonah provides a strong example of peace—giving up the need to be right and finding a sense of shalom. The book of Jonah, in chapters 1-3, describes Jonah's struggle to be right and what happens when he gives up that need. God asks Jonah to go on a mission, and Jonah refuses. Because of Jonah's insistence that he is correct, God creates a raging storm and causes Jonah to be swallowed by a big fish. It is only when Jonah practices *shalom* that he leaves the belly of the fish and continues on his way. Jonah's need to be right almost cost him his life; an extreme example but not out of line when we see what pride and egotism can cause in today's world.

There are countless opportunities during the day to practice peace, especially for children. Many of them begin with recognizing differences—either differences of opinion or difference in expectations. Some actions your child can take that show peace:

- Walking away when being teased.

- Holding your tongue when you are angry.

- Recognizing differences without judging.

- Spending time each day in prayer or thoughtful reflection.

Truthfulness (*emet*): Being truthful is a fundamental value in all religions. For children, truthfulness begins by understanding the difference between reality and

80

fantasy. We can have our fantasies, but we need to remember the difference between what is real and what we *wish* were real. Those who forget this difference create a separation between themselves and others by breaking a bond of trust. By practicing honesty, we strengthen ties to others by creating an atmosphere of positive feelings. An important teaching in Judaism is to "teach your tongue to say 'I don't know', lest you be led to lie[8]."

The book of Judges gives us great role models for speaking truthfully, among them the judge and prophet Deborah. She was respected nationwide for her honesty and ability to see the truth in all matters, and brought the Hebrews triumphantly through a tumultuous time in their history. Judges, chapter 4, shows Deborah speaking the truth about the upcoming battle, successfully predicting the success of the Hebrew armies. The entire book of Judges is about truth as told by prophets. The lesson told by this part of the Bible is that although the truth may not be popular, it is the best path to follow.

The value of truth is practiced in actions also, by living as we say we believe. Truthfulness means avoiding white lies, being honest in our business dealings (and for children, their dealings with peers), and avoiding the pressure to cheat, even when cheating is easy. Children practice this value when they:

- Remember not to exaggerate when talking about their accomplishments.

- Are honest about their own mistakes.

- Learn to find out the truth for themselves, rather than believing others.

- Remember to label stories so they are not confused with reality.

Good speech (*lashon tov*): Speaking well of another person creates good feelings, while speaking ill of them creates sourness. Some older Jewish sources make gossip

81

equivalent to murder, for unkind words "murder" a reputation. Just as killing is not reversible, so gossip can never be undone because its seeds spread too rapidly. Instead, when we look at the positive traits of each person we can spread kind words instead.

The Bible can provide us with examples of good speech, especially in the Psalms. These poems were written by King David to praise God, and have served as words for many of beautiful songs. Psalms 117 is a short, excellent example of *lashon tov*, being a song of thanksgiving to God. The familiar Psalm 23 (the lord is my shepherd) is another example, speaking about the comfort God provides to us.

Often, failure to use "good speech" results from an unresolved problem with another person. The first step then becomes having the bravery to speak to the person face to face and resolve the issue without speaking of it to others. This valuable lesson is important to teach to children. Some ways children practice good speech include:

- Walking away from a conversation that turns to gossip.

- Remembering not to repeat gossip, and not to talk behind anyone's back.

- Learning to make their own decisions about people instead of listening to gossip.

- Focusing on people's good traits.

- Work out problems directly with others, instead of resorting to gossip.

Respect (*kaved*): Each person is created in God's image, and appreciating that holiness is the essence of respect. Valuing the dignity of each individual, and learning to avoid causing embarrassment or shame is fundamental to this value. Within the family, we give an important place to respecting, or honoring, one's parents. This works both ways: we must respect our children as well, and value their rights as individuals. Talking about respect is a perfect entree to the ten commandments (Exodus chapter 20). The five commandments that pertain to other people (honoring parents, avoiding murder, adultery, false witness and covetousness) are each an example of showing respect to others. Combined with the Holiness Code, these rules for life give a well-rounded picture of what it means to respect others. Treating others with respect helps people feel valued. Being respectful includes honoring other people's property and privacy, just as we expect them to honor ours. Children practice respect in the following ways:

- Listening to their elders, and realizing they have important wisdom to provide.

- Speaking to others with courtesy.

- Treating others' property with special care.

- Remembering to knock before opening closed doors.

These eight values touch the essence of Judaism, but they could easily be joined by many others that are also important. We could add *derech eretz* (proper behavior), *pikuah nefesh* (saving life), and many others. All of these values emerge from Torah, and we cannot speak of Torah without speaking of God. Children have many questions about God, and they are some of the most difficult ones to answer. The next chapter shows how to explain some of life's puzzles to your children and grandchildren, again using Fact, Feelings, Friends, and Focus.

છ   છ   છ   છ   છ

83

7
Talking About God

"God can do anything except swim. That's be-cause spirits can't go in the water."
(Jeremy, age 8)

ભ   ભ   ભ   ભ   ભ

Explaining God to children is hard. There is no easy way to describe God, and sometimes there is no correct answer to their question. In a world filled with 30-second sound bites and quick fixes, it's hard to come up with a one-sentence response when a child asks "Why do we pray?" "Why do people get sick?" or even "Why did God create ants?" Because children of different ages see things very differently, it may be hard to understand what your child or grandchild is really asking. While a six-year-old who asks why his younger sister is sick may be wondering if the illness is his fault, a 12-year-old with the same question is more likely to be puzzling over why bad things happen to good people. Talking about these issues is so complex that it's a wonder we ever say anything at all.

One parent with an advanced degree in education feels this dilemma acutely. "I feel so lost in this area," he laments. "I *should* know how to talk about God to my two boys, but I don't even know where to start." Talking about God is probably second only to sex education in a parent's list of topics to avoid.

Because we don't have all the answers ourselves, and because we don't have language to describe something that is beyond words, we answer most of their questions with one-sentence answers that don't satisfy them or us. If we're lucky, we have a rabbi or educator who can provide part of the answer, but they're generally not around to answer the prickly follow-up questions.

"I wish I knew the answer to that" is a perfectly acceptable response to some of life's tough questions. With one short sentence you have told your child or grandchild that there's not an easy answer, and that it's OK to be puzzled about it. If you can show him that you remain faithful without knowing all the answers, then he will feel comfortable leaving unanswered problems in his own faith as well. Saying "I don't know" is another perfect way to begin a discussion about God. It says that not all questions have answers, which is one of the mysteries of God: that God knows much but tells us little.

Talking about God, prayer, or pain works best when it is tied to actual events. Looking at a dead leaf on a plant can spark a seven-year-old's interest in the impermanence of life. News stories are full of events that bring up questions about good and evil. Weekly Shabbat celebrations and holiday observances are natural openings to discuss prayer. We don't need to create ways to discuss these issues: they are all around us.

The *V'ahavtah* prayer that we recite after the *Sh'mah* includes the phrase "and teach them diligently to your children". One way to teach diligently is to teach important issues over and over; with children, once is never enough. As they grow older they become able to understand more complex problems, and questions that once were answered need to be re-explored at a deeper level. Recall we mentioned that preschool children see God as a policeman, watching over simple actions that people do to them and they do to others — a rule such as "I shouldn't hit other children" seems very straightforward to a four-year old (although it's obvious that this rule is an easy one to ignore...). When they reach school-age, the complexity of life becomes clear: "What does God want if I see someone *else* hitting?" At this point, they need to re-examine their ideas about good and evil, enriching their understanding to match their experience.

When they reach puberty and adolescence, their ability to create hypothetical scenarios makes them want to explore the issue again. Perhaps this time, the question becomes "Is it alright if a policeman is hitting a civilian?" Rather than being frustrated, parents should be encouraged when these issues are brought up repeatedly. It means that the child realizes these issues are important ones that need continual refinement and rethinking.

The Four Factors and God

When children ask these difficult questions, it helps to remember that there are four different types of answers to their questions. From the **Fact** perspective, children are looking for information and data to enlarge their understanding. Definitions, comparison examples, and any facts we can find will satisfy them. For these types of answers, a book such as "The Jewish Book of Why" is a great help. From a **Feelings** viewpoint, reassurance of God's love and support is required. Stories of God's continuing love, such as the story of Noah and the flood, satisfy their worries that God may not always love us.

For children coming from a viewpoint of **Friends**, the knowledge that God will always be with us is important. Forty years of mannah in the desert shows God's constancy, and serves to remind us that nothing we do will drive God away from us. And lastly, from a perspective of **Focus**, the fact that God has provided us with guidance and rules through Torah and Talmud is a helpful reminder. Responding to these four needs, we can describe God's nature something like this:

> *God has always been with us, and always will be*
> *here just like the forty years in the desert when*
> *God never left. This part of God we call being*
> *eternal. God will not stop being with us, and will*
> *always love and guide us just as God promised*
> *Noah after the flood. God can't do it any other*
> *way; we call this the unchanging nature of God.*

You will notice that the above description has no gender labels. From a Jewish perspective, God has both male and female qualities. We call God *Malkenu*, our King, as well as *Shekhinah*, the Bride. Although it seems natural to call God "he", our children are better served by learning about God as neither male nor female, but rather as something that combines both aspects in a richer whole. In God, we see the perfection of what we imperfectly portray in our earthly home: male and female, time and timelessness, good and evil transcend their seeming dichotomy in God. We help our children understand this by avoiding gender labels when we discuss God and God's attributes.

Children have several basic questions about God that we as parents and grandparents can help them wrestle with. They want to know:

What is God like?

Why is prayer important?

What does God want from us?

What is sin, and why is there evil in the world?

What happens in death, and why do people die?

None of these are simple questions, but neither should they be avoided. The answers to these questions take decades to understand, but we as caregivers can guide children to begin the search for their own answers. It is up to us to provide a Jewish framework; our children will enrich these beginnings as they grow older, most likely continuing the process with their own children.

"What is God like?"

> *"What does God do all day? In his rare free time, he tries to help people make decisions and talks to rabbis."* (Jeremy, age 10)
>
> 03   03   03   03   03

What is God like? What a question! It's a tough one to answer, but unfortunately is it also one of the first ones children ask. The difficulty comes because God is beyond words, and words are all we have to describe our world. When people describe God, they use a whole different vocabulary. Omniscient (all-knowing), numinous (un-knowable), and omnipotent (all-powerful) are not common every-day words. Fortunately, we can teach children about God in small portions that they can weave into a complete picture as they grow. Introducing them to the terms that describe God is a good way to begin, particularly for Fact-focused youngsters. They will enjoy learning new terms, and might appreciate a game of trying to think of something that is "almost like" God. This idea also reinforces the idea that God is greater, larger, and more than we can see in daily life.

God's love and concern for us are important concepts to most children. In young children, the tendency to think of God as a super-real parent is unavoidable, especially when we speak of a caring God. But children with an emphasis in Feeling need these reassurances. For the Friends aspect, the fact that we can never be far away from God is important. And lastly, knowing that God wants to show us the correct way and help us is a perfect introduction to Focus-oriented children. An answer that includes all of these perspectives might be:

> *Since we can't see God, we have to get ideas*
> *about God from the Torah. It's very hard to know*
> *everything about God because God is different*
> *from us. But we know that God is eternal (is*
> *always with us), omniscient (understands*
> *everything), and omnipresent (is everywhere). We*
> *also know that God loves us and wants only the*
> *best for us. God will always be with us, and tells*
> *us in the Torah how we should behave.*

We only have indirect evidence of the nature of God, but children (and even teens) readily accept the beauties of nature and the love of families as signs of God's presence. Bible stories show that God has always been present—God's conversations with Moses are especially good to show how much God cares for us.

"Why do we pray?"

> *Prayer is a search for harmony between man and*
> *God. (Solomon B. Freehof)*

> ๖ ๖ ๖ ๖ ๖

For Jewish adults, prayer is often so automatic we do it without question. When others stand, we stand. When the Sh'ma is recited, we say it as well. But children don't understand why we would "talk" to someone we can't see in a language we don't normally speak. As we saw with questions about God's character, there are four types of questions children need answered. First, they want to know why prayer is necessary (especially if they are in the **Fact** group). They are curious as to the meanings of the Hebrew words, and will enjoy hearing the translations after they learn a new prayer or blessing. Fortunately, there are many *siddurim* (prayerbooks) for children available that include translations.

Children naturally need some "how-to" guidance, and will feel proud when they can recite a blessing by themselves (especially school-age children and those in the **Focus** group). A good *Siddur* will provide enough prayers, transliterations, and translations to keep most children occupied for quite some time. Girls, especially, are attracted to the peaceful feelings that emerge from praying. Remind them that speaking their own private prayer is perfectly acceptable, and that those personal prayers do not need to be in Hebrew.

Lastly, children are comforted by knowing that Jews everywhere recite the Shabbat blessing over the candles, say the *Sh'ma* before bed, and recite *Kaddish*. This knowledge provides a sense of connection with the Jewish community, supporting the aspect of **Friends**. By providing answers to these important questions, we give children a powerful tool for connecting to their faith and to the community of believers. Here is one school-age explanation of prayer that includes all four responses:

> *Jews pray because God asked us to. Prayer is how we communicate with God, and how we thank God and sometimes ask God for things. After we pray, we feel at peace because we are connected to God. There are group prayers that we say together in a group of ten Jews, and there are very short prayers we can say by ourselves, like the Sh'ma. When we say a blessing over food, we are also thanking God for giving us so many good things. There are also special prayers that we say on holidays, Shabbat, and other special days. There are many chances to talk with God. Sometimes we can just pray using our own words, and God likes those prayers also.*

When children ask about prayer it is an excellent time to

91

teach them a new blessing. Bring out a *siddur* (prayerbook) and
see how many times you can find the familiar *"Baruch atah
Adonai"*, which signals a blessing or prayer. You can also help a
child create their own personal prayer to thank God for something
in their lives; one family created a prayer for their children to use
in school exams (Praise to God, Ruler of the Universe, who helps
us remember what we have been taught). That's creative use of
prayer!

"What does God want from us?"

Shortly after realizing that God loves us comes the
question "so, what does God want for all this love and concern?"
As children grow older they realize that there are few free rides
in life, and that God expects certain things of us in order to
maintain our connection with God. First, there are expectations
about how we treat the rest of God's creation—people, other
creatures, and the earth. Spelled out in Torah, these expectations
go hand in hand with the values we teach our children (such as
practicing <u>h</u>esed, *tzedakah*, and so forth). God also want us to
learn more about God, which will be good news to those Fact-
focused kids. God wants us to study Torah so that we learn as
much as possible about our faith; traditionally, Torah study
begins at 3 years old with fathers bringing their children to view
the Torah for the first time. The tradition of dipping a finger in
honey during the study of Torah was created so their first "taste
of Torah" would be sweet.

When children ask what God wants from us, it is a good
time to discuss the extra tasks that God gave the Jewish people.
Being God's "chosen people" means that God expects more of
us than of non-Jews. God asks us to follow more than 10
command-ments: we are also to watch what we eat, how we treat
others, and how we celebrate Shabbat and holidays. Children
learn these commandments (or *mitzvot*) by doing them—having a

Shabbat dinner, cleaning our home for Passover, or discussing our family's *tzedakah* project.

It is comforting for children to know that even when we have momentary lapses and fail to do what God expects, God does not desert us. God has promised to be with us always, and just like a parent's love it can be strained but never broken. The prayers in Psalms (for example, Psalm 116) shows us what King David believed about God's love for us: "I love the Lord for He hears my voice, my pleas; for He turns His ear to me whenever I call[9]."

God is not a school-master with hands on hips saying "I *expect* you to do these things." Rather, God *hopes* for us that we are able to live by the *mitzvot*. When we fulfill these commandments, we make our world better for ourselves and for all of God's creation. Using the four factors again, here is a brief description of God's expectations:

> *God wants us to know that we will always be loved and protected. God is always with us, even when we aren't in synagogue or praying. God also wants us to learn more about God, so God asks us to read Torah and study. God expects us to treat others with re-spect and to follow some basic rules. These commandments, or mitzvot, come from Torah.*

"What is sin, and why is there evil in the world?"

One of the most difficult tasks in life is grappling with the concept of evil. While children certainly cannot be expected to understand an issue that leaves most adults puzzled, they can be reassured that their questions are valid. The reassurance that "I wonder about that too" is helpful to young questioners. Perhaps the most valuable information we can provide to explain evil and sin is to explain what they are *not*. Often children think of evil as a punishment. The Jewish perception is quite the opposite—that bad things happen regardless of our own actions. Bad people are not the only ones who get cancer, and good people do not always have good lives. Children often feel responsible for things that are not their fault—pain and suffering should not be one of these items.

Those youngsters with an inclination towards **Facts** need extra consideration here; since the concept of evil defies logic, they are often frustrated trying to understand the concept. They find satisfaction knowing that humans have struggled with this question for centuries, and that great minds still have not found suitable answers. The **Friends** and **Feeling** groups will be helped by knowing that evil is not a sign that God has deserted us. As the Bible tells us, God always strives to be with us; sometimes it is just more difficult to hear God's voice.

From a Jewish perspective, to sin is to cut oneself off from other people and from God. Sin happens when people make bad choices, and as long as people can choose freely, they will sometimes make poor decisions. God asks only that we refrain from repeating the same bad choices over and over—that we learn from our mistakes. Here is one way to explain evil to children:

> *We don't understand why evil is in the world.*
> *Even though God loves us, there are many things*
> *that happen that are bad for people. As Jews, we*
> *don't believe that bad things are a punishment—*
> *they don't happen because we have been bad. Bad*
> *things happen to good people and to bad people.*
> *When people are evil or do bad things, Jews*
> *believe that it is because they made a poor*
> *decision. There is always a choice to do good*
> *things, and God hopes that we choose that way.*
> *But because God made us able to decide for*

*ourselves, sometimes we make a choice that hurts
ourselves or someone else.*

There are many examples we can add to the short
paragraph above. Mentioning a bad choice we made, commenting
that we don't understand and yet we still trust God, or mentioning
some good choices we have seen our children make can make the
issue more understandable. There are no easy answers here, and
the best approach is to admit our confusion.

"What is death, and why do people die?"

*The righteous servant of God loves the life of this
world merely because it serves as a step-ladder to
the next world. (Saadya Gaon)*

ઉ   ઉ   ઉ   ઉ   ઉ

When I began to write this chapter, I asked for
suggestions from several friends who work with children.
Nothing brought stronger opinions than the subject of death.
Many friends told of the trauma of losing a family member when
they were young, and most of them described feeling confused
during their period of mourning. From these comments and
shared stories, I extracted some ideas that summarized what they
most wished to pass on to those caring for children: (a) when a
child is silent it does not mean he or she is "OK"; (b) doing
nothing about a death is not a good option; and (c) children
usually know more than we think they know.

When a child doesn't talk about the death of a loved one,
it can mean many things. It often means they sense the pain of
others and don't want to add to the burden. One adult shared the
grief of losing her father three months before her bat mitzvah,
and of not feeling able to grieve because the adults around her
were in such obvious pain. Silence can also mean that they feel

responsible in some way for the death or for the pain others feel; younger children who were angry with someone when they died usually feel some sense of guilt for contributing to their death. Often, children have many questions but don't know how to phrase them, or who to ask. Rarely does silence mean that things are OK.

Children understand death in many ways. For preschool-aged children, death is not seen as final, but as a very long sleep from which the person may emerge at some point in the future. Most psychologists agree that there is little benefit in bringing preschool or kindergarten children to funerals. Younger school-age children understand that death is final, but before age ten or so they don't see death as inevitable. These children believe death happens to some people, but not necessarily to all. It is not until nine or ten years of age that we know death as the ultimate end for each of us.

Regardless of the aspect of faith a child follows, there are ways to deal with death that will bring a sense of closure to a child and allow children to move ahead with their lives. The Jewish way is just that: to mourn for a time, and then to continue with life. **Focus**-oriented and **Friends**-focused children need to perform some physical act that brings the life of the departed into focus. The action can be a visit to the gravesite, a letter to the departed person, or some ritual that had meaning to the family. In addition, children who emphasize Friends will be comforted by being with family and friends during this important time. These children do not handle grief well if left alone. Focus-oriented children will be comforted by following mourning rituals; they will find comfort in following the expectations to sit Shiva, go to the graveside, and participate in other traditions of Jewish bereavement.

Fact-focused children, especially older ones, will want to understand the Jewish perception of what happens after death (there are several good sources for this information, presented in Chapter 9.) They often need to talk about the departed person, for talking allows them a way to make sense of their emotions. Children with a **Feelings** perspective need to be able to express their emotions and to talk to a sympathetic listener. Feeling-oriented children need to understand that grief is a natural reaction to death, and not anything to be ashamed of. Children don't understand that the grief will lessen in time, but sharing your own experiences with death helps them to see that others have coped and moved on with their lives.

In retrospect, adults talking about childhood losses say that they were not surprised when an sick person died. Hushed voices, sad faces and changes in routine often provide all the clues a child needs to understand the severity of the situation. Adults need not be afraid to tell a child that a person is dying, as it generally confirms what they already sense. Children who are facing death themselves seem to know it also; they don't speak of it because they know it brings their family pain. In as gentle a way as possible we can find out what the child already knows, and then fill in the rest of the picture as best we can.

God made the world so that everything dies. People, animals, even plants all die. We don't know what happens to people after they die, since they can't tell us. But the Jewish idea of death is that we each have a soul that continues to live after our body is gone. Since those of us who are still living can't see this soul, we miss the person and we feel sad. It takes people different amounts of time to stop feeling sad, and when we don't feel so sad we can still remember the person and think of good times we had with them. Jews bury a person's body in the ground, and then other Jews help the family that is left behind by going to their house and bringing them food. The family also says a special prayer each day, and there are seven days where the family usually stays at home. Then the family slowly starts to go back to its regular activities. That is the Jewish way.

Children are often comforted to know that others have gone through the pain of loss. Sharing your own stories of bereavement give children models to follow *and* allows you to honor the memory of the departed. In Jewish tradition it is *good* to speak of those no longer with us, because it keeps their memory alive. By remembering them, we help them to live among us.

ೞ   ೞ   ೞ   ೞ   ೞ

Children's questions are many, and we have touched on but a few. Whatever the question, the best answer is one that touches on Jewish tradition (what we do) and Jewish belief (what we know), sprinkled with a bit of our own feelings. The next chapter addresses more of these frequently-asked questions, this time focusing on holidays and customs. In the next chapter, we will dig into these issues using the factors of faith as our guide.

8
Those Nasty FAQ's (Frequently Asked Questions)

To question is to open a door to faith. (Anonymous)

೮ঃ   ೮ঃ   ೮ঃ   ೮ঃ   ೮ঃ

In every family there are certain discussions that never seem to end, often becoming the basis for minor weekly battles. When I was growing up, at least once a week my brother would ask "Do I have to brush my teeth tonight? With toothpaste?" Of course our mother would always answer affirmatively to both questions, and I remember silently mouthing the "with toothpaste" question along with him (I knew the rhythm of his words, and can hear it in my head to this day). Whether due to a sensitive mouth or a dislike for mint, we never learned. But his repeated questions, like others in your own families, mark an underlying unanswered question. Just as a peanut butter sandwich can never satisfy us if we are craving Campbell's tomato soup, the 'wrong' answer never leaves us fully satisfied.

Many questions that our children ask about Judaism fall into this category. We answer the "presenting" question ("Why do

I have to go to Hebrew school today?" "Because I'm driving the carpool."), but leave the underlying issue unresolved. Sometimes we don't understand what our children are really asking, but other times we're not sure how to give them the explanation that will work *for them*. Depending upon your child's primary inclination, there are alternative ways to answer each question of faith. The **Facts** group is mostly interested in gathering information and understanding why or how things are as they are. But this information is incredibly boring to the **Feelings** folks, who want to understand the emotions associated with a particular issue or to be reassured that things really are OK. **Friends**-focused children are interested in shared ideas or events that will bring them into community with others, and **Focus**-oriented people are looking for directions or to do what is expected; "if God expects it, we'll do it".

A child's age also affects the type of answer that will be most helpful; children will ask the same question several times between toddlerhood and adulthood, demanding more complex answers as their comprehension expands. Just when they seem to "get it", they think of a new twist on an old question. (I remember my brother asking, at a later age, why toothpaste was necessary to keep teeth clean since we spit it out anyway.) Despite the frustration these repeat questions can cause, they can be the entree to important conversations that touch the very soul of the Jewish faith.

Matzoh Again(!?) ...or, Why Kashrut?

Jewish dietary laws, or *kashrut*, are one of the defining characteristics of the Jewish people. Recent surveys find that the majority of Jewish households observe dietary restrictions of some sort, from full *kashrut* to "kosher style." The range is varied: some families forbid pork dishes and shellfish and do not address other restrictions. Others observe at home but not when they are in non-Jewish surroundings. Still others are fully observant, with two sets of dishes, silverware, and mixing bowls. Regardless of the level of observance in your home, there will be times when the Jewish diet is at odds with the American way of eating. At some point your child will notice the difference between your family's eating habits and those of their friends, and an important "teachable moment" arrives.

Many explanations have been given for Jewish dietary laws and *Pesadikh* practices. To a school-aged child, most of them are not responsive to the real question, which is more along the lines of "why me?" than "which foods?". The **Fact**-focused child is looking for a logical explanation, and he won't be satisfied with the older explanations regarding pork causing disease. One powerful reason for the "no pork or shellfish" requirement is actually a non-reason. It goes something like this: "There is more to being faithful than just understanding, and so some things we are asked to do don't have a logical reason. Some things (like avoiding pork) we do just because God asks us, not because they make sense." This anti-logic explanation is surprisingly enticing to children coming from a perspective of Fact. Since trying to understand the reason for *kashrut* is difficult, we do an end run on the process by admitting there does not seem to be any logic. A Fact-focused child will often develop his own logical explanation, and be quite proud of figuring out something that adults have trouble with.

Children in the **Feelings** and **Focus** categories need another type of explanation entirely. These boys and girls are looking for an impact on daily life, and they can appreciate that keeping kosher is an ideal way for this involvement to take place. For them, the answer goes something like "Keeping dietary laws brings holiness to an act that all of us do every day. If we think about what we eat, and know that God has "approved" each mouthful, we bring God with us to the breakfast table, the grocery store, and cafeteria lunch lines." One mother always brings one child with her to the grocery store to help her read the labels to avoid mixing milk with meat products.

Yet another explanation for kosher eating satisfies the child whose focus is on **Friends**. The laws of *kashrut* have been the same for centuries, and maintaining these laws is a way of tying us to the Jewish community throughout history. When we know that Jews all over the world are cleaning their house of leaven in preparation for Passover, or break the fast after sundown on *Yom Kippur*, we feel a tie to them and the whole of Judaism.

Combining all four responses into one response might go something like this: Why do we observe *kashrut*? "We don't know why God wants us to observe these laws, but we know that it reminds us of God all day long. Jews everywhere observe the same diet, and it ties us to the rest of the Jewish community."

Why Can't I go to Soccer Practice... or...What's so special about Shabbat?

Shabbat is another defining characteristic of a Jewish lifestyle. Here again families make different choices as to the level of observance, but all have the same emphasis on time "set apart" from the rest of the week. Children enjoy the regularity of Shabbat observance; even teens often enjoy lighting the Shabbat candles. One mother with a three-year-old daughter remarked that every time she dresses her daughter in a dress, her daughter asks "are we going to *shul*?" They are regulars at Saturday morning services and her daughter is clearly eager to go. Another pair of grandparents always has Shabbat dinner waiting on the table at 6:30; one or the other of their three children (and grandchildren) always seems to drop by unexpectedly at just about 6pm—just in time for dinner.

But as children grow there are many activities that pull

102

families towards non-observance. Friday night movies with
friends, Saturday soccer practice, and play or dance rehearsals
are common in most families. The key to maintaining some
observance of Shabbat is to make a decision, communicate it to
the rest of the family, and stick to it. If you decide to allow
Saturday soccer practice, perhaps you can insist on Shabbat
dinner the night before. One family keeps strict Shabbat until
noon on Saturday (including Torah study as a family), after
which other activities are allowed. But oddly enough, the mother
of this family says that "my kids seem to hang around a long
time after noon—it's almost as if they don't want to let go of
Shabbat". If you decide to commit to a complete day of rest,
make a family decision about what is considered work (not
permitted) and what is permitted. For example, driving may be
acceptable if it is to take a family outing.

　　Whatever level of observance you choose, your children
will need reasons for the celebration of Shabbat. Here again the
faith aspects can help us speak to the underlying question. For
children relating to **Feelings**, Shabbat is most easily seen as a
"refreshment break", where the stresses of the week are set aside
and we focus instead on our faith. Describing Shabbat as a day
of Jewish study will be most appealing to those **Fact**-focused
children who need little excuse to plunge into a book. **Friends**-
focused kids will appreciate the opportunity to be with friends
and family in activities, while those most **Focus**-oriented
understand the day as a commandment—when we celebrate
Shabbat we are doing what God expects of us. One explanation
that includes all of these is that "Shabbat is a gift from God to all
Jews when we can relax, be with family and friends, and learn
more about our faith."

　　Shabbat is enriching for each of us no matter what our
orientation. Be sure that your family has the opportunity to
experience Shabbat peace as fully as possible.

Where's our Christmas Tree...or...How Are Jews Different?

One of the most troublesome set of questions deals with the comparison of Judaism to other religions. Often these questions revolve around holiday celebrations such as Christmas and Easter, both of which occur close to Jewish holidays. For years one mother got away with a very simple explanation: "How can we celebrate Christmas? We just got through *Hanukkah!*" When these non-explanations no longer suffice, we need to present a more satisfying reason for the differences between our celebrations and Christian holidays. As early as possible, tolerance for religious differences can be encouraged. While preschoolers cannot understand the theological differences between religions, they can certainly understand that families practice differently because they were taught differently. And that being different is just that—not better or worse, just different.

Children with an emphasis on **Focus** perhaps require the least explanation for the difference in holidays. They understand when we tell them that Jews have another set of rules to live by, and that we don't celebrate holidays that are Christian just as they do not celebrate the Jewish holidays. When children are older, parents can add more explanation along a **Fact**-based line: that we don't celebrate the birth or death of Jesus because we don't think he was the savior of the world. Children coming from a Fact emphasis will also appreciate a more thorough explanation of the difference between Judaism and Christianity—that we await the *Meshiah* (Messia) or the Messianic age, while Christians think that it has already come.

For those with a basis in **Feelings**, it helps to talk about being uncomfortable in other people's celebrations, and the happiness (and fun) that our Jewish celebrations bring. Children emphasizing **Friends** can be directed to the feelings of community that we feel spending holidays with those who believe as we do. When we celebrate other people's holidays, we do so as an outsider and not as a member of the group.

Some holidays, such as Christmas and Easter, are obviously non-Jewish holidays. Others are much more subtle, and warrant a family decision on whether and how to celebrate the holiday. St. Valentine's Day and Halloween are two such days — both are Roman Catholic in origin. It is very difficult for children to avoid celebrating these holidays short of staying home from school, and in fact that is what some families choose. Other families put a Jewish twist on them, suggesting costumes of biblical characters for Halloween (how about Mordecai and Esther?), and avoiding the giving of Valentine cards but instead give tzedakah in the name of their classmates. Whatever the family's choice, it should be a conscious one and not decided by default.

Why Aren't the Prayers in English... or... Why study Hebrew?

Hebrew, the language of the Torah, is a living language because of a modern-day miracle. Like Latin, Hebrew was in danger of becoming a language known only to scholars. But when it became the State of Israel's official language, Hebrew became again a language that lived outside of the prayerbook.

To say a prayer in Hebrew gives the prayer special significance. It goes without saying that God hears prayers in all languages, and yet praying in Hebrew (even if only reading the English transliteration) brings a special connection to the rest of the Jewish community. The rabbis believed that the Hebrew language existed before the beginning of the world, and that God used the aleph-bet to begin creation. If that is so, it seems that the preservation of the Hebrew language is a mitzvah of sorts;

learning at least a bit of Hebrew is a way of preserving the world and renewing the work of creation.

But learning a language is difficult, and with Hebrew comes the double task of learning new words *and* new symbols. Most children at one time or other complain about learning Hebrew (if your child does not, give yourself brownie points for early indoctrination!). Your child sooner or later will ask why it is required, and again there are several ways to respond. **Fact**-oriented children will be interested to know that the subtleties of Hebrew don't translate well into English; in order to thoroughly understand Torah passages they should be read in the original language of Hebrew. Hebrew is a significant part of our tradition that connects us to other Jews, which will provide a satisfying answer to children in the **Friends** and **Focus** categories. And the beauty of the language, particularly as calligraphy in some early Passover *Haggadot*, will satisfy the aesthetic sensibilities of the **Feelings**-oriented child.

Do I *really* have to go to services?...or...Why follow rituals?

Kelly is a spunky nine-year-old who has no trouble out-talking most adults. Ask her a question, and more than likely she will come up with an answer *and* a story to illustrate her point. Kelly had difficulty sitting quietly through an entire Shabbat service until she went to services with her grandmother one day. When Kelly began to squirm, her grandmother told her "Shhhh, God wants us to listen!" Since that time Kelly has declined several invitations with friends because God "expects" her in services. The pull of ritual is strong for many of us; we, like Kelly, fulfill many mitzvot simply because "God expects us to." Jewish life is rich with ritual—there are rituals that mark daily activities, weeks and months, holidays, and life events. It has often been said that ritual is *the* most critical feature of Judaism;

we don't have a common creed but we have standard acts in which we are expected to participate. So for many of us, there is no reason necessary for performing rituals—we just do them. Others, including many children, need some sort of justification for a particular ritual act. There are, of course, standard generic answers that apply to each ritual: God requires us to do them (**Focus**), they create a connection to others in the Jewish community (**Friends**), and they comfort us (**Feelings**). Yet children deserve a deeper answer as well that touches on the heart of the specific ritual. **Fact**-oriented children will be most interested in these answers, while all children as they grow older require at least a brief explanation. Here is a brief list of Jewish rituals and their "reasons" that you can share with your children. These are only some of the many rituals in Jewish life; the resources you will find later in Chapter 9 can give you more detail and additional examples.

Daily prayers...remind us that God is with us always.

Fasting on *Yom Kippur*....is commanded in Torah.

Kissing a *mezuzah*/Torah...is a sign of respect and reverence.

Saying an additional prayer (*kiddush*) on Shabbat... reinforces the holiness of the day.

Wearing *tallit*...reminds us to observe God's laws.

Blowing the *shofar*...reminds us of God's gift of Torah.

Standing during prayers...shows respect to God.

Women lighting Shabbat candles...allows women to bring redemption to the world.

Circumcision...is commanded in Torah as a sign of God's covenant with the Jews.

Lighting candles for *Yahrzeits*...symbolizes the soul (flame) reaching upward.

Covering the *challah* on Shabbat...is covering the (Shabbat) bride's face at a wedding.

Wearing a *yarmulke/kipah*...is a sign of reverence for

God.

Lighting more than one candle on Shabbat...reminds us of Shabbat's many blessings.

Elijah's cup on the Passover table...symbolizes our hope that the messiah will come soon.

Building a *sukkah* with an open ceiling...reminds us of the Israelites in the desert.

Adding candles each day of Hanukkah...reminds us that God's blessings increase.

While these "explanations" are traditional, many other interpretations are possible. One family has a contest each holiday to come up with the best new explanation for a ritual. The winning idea is written down, and a new winner is added every year. This way the children get more involved with the holiday, and the explanations add to everyone's understanding of Jewish tradition.

Why do we wear the Star of David...or...What is the State of Israel?

For many Jews today, the State of Israel is a powerful symbol. It symbolizes the Jewish people and our ability to arise phoenix-like from adversity. It represents the land to which we wish to return (or visit) before we die. To children, it often represents an unknown, mysterious place that they know little about. While it appears on countless posters and appears in dozens of Hebrew school lessons, it remains a vague place in the mind of most youngsters. One obvious solution exists: have them visit Israel. For many teens, a visit to Israel creates a powerful connection to Judaism. The combination of time away from home, bonding with peers, and the incomparable nature of Israel and Jerusalem makes an impact on even the most reticent of teenagers. While there are certainly signs of unrest and modernization in Israel, signs of Jewish roots permeate Jerusalem, creating an indelible impression on the minds of young Jews. Giving your child (or grandchild) a trip to Israel is one way to assure the continuation of the Jewish people and the perpetuation of the Jewish State of Israel.

Until your children can visit, they must be content with your explanations of our ties to Israel. They need a sense of its history (biblical to modern) and an understanding of its central focus as the spiritual home of the Jews—even those who do not live there. Fact-focused children will be most interested in history books, while the other three groups will be more satisfied by understanding Israel as the Jewish homeland. The fact that it is the only nation to have Hebrew as its national language also creates an important link between Jews and Israel. If donations to Israel and prayers for Jerusalem are important to you, let your children see you write the check and hear you pray the prayer. As their most important role model, you can influence their future relationship to the Jewish homeland.

What is that tattoo on Uncle's arm...or...What was the Holocaust?

As difficult as it may be, children need some understanding of the Holocaust. For many parents, the words are impossible to utter. The horror is too close, often in our own families. The *Shoah* is impossible to explain, and difficult to describe. *Baruch Hashem* (thank God), there are now memorials in most major cities that can do the job for us. Many movies have been made that describe various aspects of this piece of Jewish history; if you choose to explain the Holocaust in this manner be sure to watch the movie with your children. There are many books available for older children, but they again should only be offered as an additional resource after some initial explanation from a caring adult.

109

Specific descriptions of the atrocities are not particularly necessary, and very difficult to take especially for the more sensitive. As we continue to heal from this all-too-recent tragedy, Jews can bring valuable lessons to the rest of humanity and continue on the path of *tikkun olam*, healing the world. Children can appreciate that even in the most difficult of circumstances valuable lessons arise. Because the Shoah literally decimated the Jewish community, children can understand that strengthening Judaism is important now that our numbers are less. And since we have struggled through countless horrors, Jewish adults and children can ensure that the term "never again" applies to all humankind. Compassion for the downtrodden can come from the Jewish community after being treated with kindness by hundreds of "righteous gentiles". These are lessons we should teach all our children, whatever their approach to faith.

Why didn't Nannah go to the wedding...or...Why not intermarry?

Most Jewish adults rank the preservation of Judaism very highly, and the fact that 50% of modern Jewish marriages are to non-Jews strikes fear in the hearts of many parents and grandparents. Keeping our children out of that statistical pile can become a major driving force to parents, especially as their children enter the dating years.

I must admit to an ambivalence on this point. While I am absolutely committed to the survival of the Jewish religion, I honestly do not see intermarriage as the issue. Instead, I see *lack of commitment to Judaism* as the essential problem. Whether they are married to Jews or non-Jews, or not married at all, *our children will not contribute to Judaism's survival without a commitment to their faith.* The entire thesis of this book is to demonstrate how to bring your child into a true connection with

Judaism. If/when that is accomplished, marriage or intermarriage becomes a moot point. Adults who are committed to their faith do *not* turn away from religion or raise their children in a different faith.

The flip side of the inter-marriage statistic is the conversion statistic. The greatest increase to the Jewish community in the past several decades has not been through births, but through conversion. While not all converts to Judaism arise from interfaith marriages, a majority of them do. Quite frankly, the best way to increase the Jewish population is to marry a non-Jew, show your spouse how wonderful the Jewish faith is, and make them want to become Jewish! But again, in order for this scenario to work, it takes a *commitment to Judaism.*

A firm commitment to Judaism can also lead to a commitment to marry *only* another Jew. For some, a strong commitment to Judaism leads naturally to choosing a Jewish spouse since they cannot envision being coupled for life to a person of a different faith. The popularity of Jewish singles organizations speaks to the truth of this statement; many Jewish singles will only consider dating Jewish women (or men) because they cannot see themselves being comfortable with a non-Jewish wife (or husband). For each of these young adults, the tie began much earlier when their families showed them the value of Judaism. Now, years later, their parents can sit back and enjoy their adult children, knowing that their early lessons have born fruit.

      ୬   ୬   ୬   ୬   ୬

These eight "frequently-asked questions" provide examples of ways to emphasize the core values and expectations of Judaism. There are most certainly other issues that will arise in your home, and your responses can be patterned along the guidelines offered here. Remember to include a bit of fact, some emotions, and shared experiences to your explanations, and your children will find value in your answers. "But," you say, "there are hundred of questions, and I don't have all the answers!" Help is on the way. In the next chapter, you will find dozens of ideas and resources to use in your family. Even a two-Ph.D. family will never know the answers to all of the questions kids can ask, so make liberal use of the resources in the next chapter and experience a leap forward in your family's interest in things Jewish.

9
Resources & Ideas for Each Age Child

C3   C3   C3   C3   C3

We have examined the specifics of each age and each approach to faith, it's now time to put these ideas together in a useable format. This chapter lists activities that your child can do by himself or with friends to grow in faith and spirituality; the following chapter includes suggestions for family participation. Over 150 resources and their sources are listed below, along with suggestions as to which faith aspect they serve best. Facts, Feelings, Friends and Focus are listed as Fa, Fe, Fr, and Fo; you will notice that many resources are appropriate for more that one group.

The listings here are meant to spark your own investigation of the materials available; it attempts include at least one resource in each category of Jewish life, ritual and belief. There are hundreds more listings that could have been included, and their absence should not be taken as lack of endorsement. If you cannot find these materials at your local Judaica shop, most are available from the manufacturer or publisher, and many through internet sources.

Preschool Resources

Books: There are literally hundreds of read-aloud books that are superb for children of this age. In addition to instilling a love of books, reading Jewish books together is an important way to instill a love of Judaism in young children. Here are just a few of the many options:

Annie's Shabbat, Sarah Marwil Lamstein, Cecily Lang (illust). Albert Whitman & Co., 1997. (about $16) Named a "Top Ten Religious Book", the description of a family Shabbat is enriched with cut rice-paper illustrations. A special book to keep for many years. (Fe, Fr, Fo)

Bible Heroes I Can Be, Ann Eisenberg, Rosalyn Schanzer (illust). Kar-Ben Books, 1990. (about $9). Tells stories of Biblical figures, and shows what children can do and say to follow in their footsteps. (Fo)

Blessed Are You—Traditional Everyday Hebrew Prayers, Michelle Edwards. Lothrop, Lee & Shephard, 1993. (about $15) Richly illustrated book of thirteen traditional prayers and blessings. (Fa, Fe)

But Then I Remembered, Chaya Leah Rothstein. Feldheim Publishers, 1991. (about $12). How their grandparents act help these children choose the right path to follow. (Fo)

God's Paintbrush, Sandy Eisenberg Sasso, Annette Compton (illust). Jewish Lights Publishers, 1993. (about $17). A book full of questions that will encourage children to think about God's work in their own lives. Beautifully illustrated. (Fe, Fo)

In the Beginning, Miriam Ramsfelder Levin, Katherine Janus

114

Kahn (illust.). Kar-Ben Books, 1994. (about $15) "Adam woke up. It was dark and cold outside and he was alone. He turned on his light and surveyed his room, and saw that it was good." What a great way to make the creation story come to life! (Fa, Fo)

It Happened in Shushan, Harriet Feder. Kar-Ben Books, 1988. (about $4). The Purim story retold in a comical rebus style. Much fun! (Fr)

Jalapeno Bagels, Natasha Wing, Robert Casilla (illust.). Athenum, 1996. (About $16). A bi-cultural youngster resolves his dilemma of what to bring to International Day at school.

Let's Go to Synagogue, Ceil & David Olivestone. SBS Publishing, 1981. (about $10) Step-by-step guide to the Shabbat morning service, with bright illustrations. (Fa, Fe)

The Mouse in the Matzah Factory, Francine Medoff. Kar-Ben Books, 1983. (about $6). A mouse finds out how matzah is made. (Fa)

My Very Own Haggadah, Judyth Groner and Madeline Wikler. Kar-Ben Books, 1983. (about $3). In print for 25 years, but with new pictures for a new generation. A great first book that children will use year after year. (All)

A Purim Story, Linda Davis. Feldheim Publishers, 1988. (about $10). Brightly illustrated, the book tells the traditional story in rhyme. (Fa, Fo)

Seven Animal Stories for Children, Howard & Mary Bogot. Pitspopany Press, 1997. (about $10). One great story for each day of the week, including ideas on how to take the seven values into daily life. (Fo)

Ten Good Rules, Susan Remick Topek. Kar-Ben Books, 1992. (about $6). Pastel illustrations show Moses perched on small fingers, listing the ten commandments. (Fa, Fo)

Thank You, God!: A Jewish Child's Book of Prayers, Judyth Groner. Kar-Ben Books, 1993. (about $17). Over 20 traditional prayers in Hebrew, English, and transliteration. Wonderful illustrations show prayers that can be used every day. (Fe, Fo)

A Treasury of Jewish Bedtime Stories, Shmuel Blitz. Mesorah Publications, 1996. (about $15) Large illustrations decorate the pages filled with stories of famous rabbis and leaders. (Fa, Fo)

Very First Board Books, Kar-Ben Books. (about $5, or $55 for 13). Board books on the holidays, including It's Rosh Hashanah!, In the Synagogue, and eleven other colorful titles. (All)

Puzzles and Games: When parents make Judaism a natural part of every-day life, children grow to love their cultural heritage. One great way to accomplish this goal is to have a few toys with an obvious Jewish focus. Here are a few of the many options available:

David & Goliath Floor Puzzle, about $13. Available from *The Source for Everything Jewish,* this activity gives pre-readers an idea of the historical past. One of many toys and games that tell stories Biblical characters. (Fa)

Wooden "Shabbat Shalom" set, available from *The Source for Everything Jewish*. (about $14). Introduces children to the

Shabbat ritual through role play. (Fa)

Jewish Holiday Crafts for Little Hands, Ruth Esrig Brinn, Katherine Kahn (illus). Kar-Ben Books, 1993. (about $13). Over 100 projects for holidays and Shabbat, including Purim costumes, snacks to make, games to play. (All)

Set of Seven Fun Books, Kar-Ben Books. (about $4 each, or $27 the set.) Packed with activities, games and picture stories for seven holidays. (Fr, Fo)

Activities: Hands-on pastimes that encourage them to be creative can also be fun for this age child. Get (or make) some ritual objects that are sturdy enough to be used by a four-year-old and still last for several years. Some ideas are: (Fe, Fo)

- Purim groggers (wood lasts longer than sheet metal)

- Hannukiah with animals or other "fun" shapes (make it their hannukiah, even if you have other "grown-up" versions.)

- Small ram's horn or shofar (again, make it sturdy)

School-Age Resources

Books: As we submerge ourselves in the information age, children can be tempted to ignore "old fashioned" resources such as books. It seems that paper and ink will never be as alive as video or interactive websites, according to our children. *Au contraire*— quite the contrary! Is there any parent or grandparent who never stayed up late trying to find out how Tom Sawyer or Nancy Drew or Tom Swift solved a problem? Or missed a television show because the short story was just too engrossing to put down? The mere fact that you have purchased this book (and managed to read over 100 pages) says that you value books and reading. The way to ensure that your children value literature as well is to stock their bookshelves liberally and often. While my daughter was growing up we made frequent trips to the bookstore, and each trip that I bought a book I allowed her to choose one also. She now has quite an impressive library, and I consider my efforts a success in that as a teen she will actually spend her *own* money buying books. Beginning as early as possible, be sure that your child (or grandchild) experiences the pleasures of reading.

All About Sukkot, Judith Saypol Groyner, Madeline Wikler, Kenny Kreiswirth (illust). Kar-Ben Books, 1998.(about $5). Explains the history, customs and symbols of the feast of booths. With blessings and songs, lavishly illustrated. (Fa)

America: The Jewish Experience, Sondra Leiman, Jonathan D. Sarna (Ed.). UAHC Press, 1994. (about $12). Full of facts and information, a meticulously-researched history of Jews in America from the 1600s to the present. An excellent resource for children interested in history and "how things got to be the way they are." (Fa)

Angelicum, Lynn Sharon. Pitspopany Press, 1999. (about $10). Jewish science fiction tells of angels and impending danger. (Fa, Fe)

Bar Mitzvah : A Jewish Boy's Coming of Age, Eric A. Kimmel, Puffin Books, 1997. (about $5) Full of history, explanations and personal stories, including a memorable anecdote of a Holocaust bar mitzvah. For non-Jewish children also. (All)

Brainteasers from Jewish Folklore, Rosalind Charney Kaye. Kar-Ben Books, 1997. (about $13) A well-illustrated collection of folk riddles from Jewish tradition. Will tax the brain of children and adults. (Fa)

Blessed Are You: Traditional Everyday Hebrew Prayers, Michelle Edwards. Lothrop Lee & Shephard, 1993. (about $15). Thirteen prayers are presented in English, Hebrew and transliteration. Many illustrations make this book fun for children, with pictures showing when the particular prayers might be said (at mealtimes or in the evening, for example.) (Fe)

The Book of Miracles: A Young Person's Guide to Jewish Awareness, Lawrence Kushner. Jewish Lights Publishers, 1997. (about $17). Rabbi Kushner gives wonderful examples of how children can "find the sacred in the mysterious and beautiful occurrences of everyday lives." An excellent way to show children that God is indeed everywhere. (Fe)

Clouds of Glory: Jewish Legends & Stories About Bible Times, Miriam Chaikin. Clarion Books, 1998. (about $19.00) Remarkable for its interesting illustrations (reminiscent of stained glass) and male/female images of God, the book tells stories of God and angels from Midrash and other ancient sources. (Fe, Fo)

Classic Bible Stories for Jewish Children, Rabbi Alfred J. Kolatch. Jonathan David Publishers, 1993. (about $15) Stories of many biblical characters, nicely illustrated. (Fa)

The Energizing Jewish Holidays for Children, Gedalia Peterseil. Pitspopany Press, 1998. (about $8). Hidden holiday symbols are interspersed throughout descriptions of each holiday. A high-energy look at the Jewish year. (All)

Esther's Story, Diane Wolkstein. William Morrow & Company, 1996. (about $15.00) Written as a personal diary, the well-known story of Ester and Mordecai is retold in vivid, personal language. Wonderfully illustrated. (Fa, Fe, Fo)

Fins and Scales: A Kosher Tale, Deborah Miller and Karen Ostrove. Kar-Ben Books, 1991. (about $6) Comic rhyme explains dietary laws. A great introduction for beginning readers, and sure to stay with them over the years. (Fa)

For Kids—Putting God on Your Guest List : How to Claim the Spiritual Meaning of Your Bar/Bat Mitzvah, Jeffrey K. Salkin. Jewish Lights Publishing, 1998. (about $15) A welcome companion to the parent's volume (Putting God on the Guest List), this combination of Torah, folklore, history, theology, and liturgy helps prepare preteens spiritually for bar/bat mitzvah. (All)

Israel: The Founding of a Modern Nation, Maida Silverman, illustrations by Susan Avishai. Dial Books for Young Readers, 1998. (about $15) Beginning with God's promise to Abraham and ending with modern day Jerusalem, this well-illustrated volume provides an excellent accounting of this important part of Jewish history. (Fa)

Jerusalem 3000: Kids Discover the City of Gold, Alan Paris. Pitspopany Press, 1998. (about $17) Includes a timeline of 3,000 years of history, presented in an engaging style with tons of facts and many illustrations. (Fa)

The Jewish Children's Bible, Sheryl Prenszlau. Pitspopany Press, 1996. (about $19 ea). Five volumes cover important themes from the books of the Torah. (All)

Jewish Question Collection, Linda Schwartz, Learning Works, 1994. (about $8) Hundreds of questions on people, places, Jewish history and more. Perfect for family games or travel diversion, will keep kids (and adults) guessing for hours. (Fa, Fo)

The Jewish Storyteller Series, Kar-Ben Books. (about $17 each). Each volume has ten stories around a different theme such as classic stories, traditional stories, etc. Thoughtful questions after each story highlight the story's main theme. (Fa, Fo)

Jews in Sports, Joseph Hoffman. Pitspopany Press, 1998. (about $17) Sports heroes up to the present day in soccer, baseball, tennis, etc. (Fo)

A Kid's Catalog of Israel, Chaya Burstein. Jewish Publication Society, 1998. (about $17). This "catalog" is packed with history, customs in modern-day Israel, and stories. A good way to put the history of Israel in perspective. (Fa)

King Solomon and the Queen of Sheba, Blu Greenberg & Linda Tarry. Pitspopany Books, 1998. (about $17) Bringing cross-cultural themes into Jewish tradition, tells the story two inspiring characters. Dolls are also available. (Fo)

The Little Midrash Says, Rabbi Moshe Weissman. B'nay Yakor Publications, 1988. (about $17). One volume for each book of the Torah, with lots of extra material on customs, explanations and learning questions. A good way to learn traditions while learning Torah. (Fa)

Listen to the Trees : Jews and the Earth, Molly Cone. UAHC Press, 1998. (about $15) One of the few books to address the issue of Jews and the environment. Provides Torah's ideas of nature through quotations and stories—engaging reading for children concerned about their world. (Fe, Fo)

Menorahs, Mezuzas, and Other Jewish Symbols, Miriam Chaikin. Clarion Books, 1990. (about $17) Provides background on a wide variety of symbols and their use in ritual. A great reference for interested children. (Fa, Fo)

Na'ar Hayisi: I Was a Child, Aidel Wajngort, Norman Nodel (illust). Hachai Publishing, 1990. (about $9) Dozens of short stories about Jewish leaders as children and young people. A wealth of examples of what Jewish life can be like. (Fo, Fa)

The Shabbat Book: A Weekly Guide for the Whole Family. Based on the video, Shalom Shabbat. (about $16) Each week has its own page, with information on customs, weekly readings, and stories. Entertaining for families to use together. (Fa)

Sharing Blessings: Children's Stories for Exploring the Spirit of the Jewish Holidays, Rahel Musleah and Rabbi Michael Klayman. Jewish Lights Publications, 1997. (about $19). This unique way of presenting values tells a contemporary story for each Jewish holiday and ties it to a value, for example Sukkot and peace, Pesach and continuity, etc. (Fo)

Sidrah Stories: A Torah Companion, Steven Rosman. UAHC Press (Reform), 1989. (185 pages, about $7). A commentary on each weekly Torah portion, with questions that bring modern relevance. A great introduction to Torah study. (Fa)

The Story Hour, David Sholom Pape (Ed.), Yosef Dershowitz (illust), Davide Berg (illust). Hachai Publications, 1994. (about $12 per volume) Two volumes of Jewish tales told with humor and a sense of adventure. Vividly illustrated for beginning readers. (Fr)

Tell Me a Mitzvah, Danny Siegel. Kar-Ben Books, 1993. (about $8). Stories about "regular" people who are helping to repair the world. Important concepts for all children. (All)

Yom Kippur: A Family Service, Judith Z. Abrams. Kar-Ben Books, 1990. (about $4). Along with volumes for S'lichot and Rosh Hashanah, these prayer books are good for new readers and older children as well. (Fe, Fr)

Games and activities: Regardless of their primary faith factor, most school-age children enjoy being active. Here are some of the options for "packaged" activities; of course home-grown versions are just as good. Consider putting on a family "Purimspiel" or creating a puppet show to tell a holiday story.

Imagine...Exploring Israel, Marji and Michael Gold-Vukson. Kar-Ben Books, 1993. (about $4) Lots of "drawing adventures" for young readers. (Fa, Fr)

Jewish IQ Basketball (Windows 95). (about $35) This trivia-style game offers team or individual versions, point are collected for answering questions on Jewish history, Bible, prayer, etc. (Fa)
Matzah Meals, Judy Tabs and Barbara Steinberg. Kar-Bem Books, 1985. (about $7). A spiral-bound book chock-full of Pesadich goodies to make. (All)

My Very Own Jewish Calendar, Judyth Groner and Madeline Wikler. Kar-Ben Books. (about $7). A sixteen-month calendar with funny and informative facts and Jewish trivia. Good for a bedroom wall. (Fa, Fo)

Internet Sources:
Judaism.com.kids (www.judaism.kids.com) A page (with sounds!) containing stories, a place to become a "net pal", and links to other organizations. Also contains book reviews written for parents. (Fa)

ZigZagWorld (www.zigzagworld.com) featuring "The Best Jewish Games on the Web", lots of creative fun, as well as a resource for learning Hebrew. (Fa)

Preteen Resources

Middle-school children are very focused on finding friends and role models. The resources listed here emphasize these concerns and provide ways for Jewish preteens to identify with Judaism. To provide your own preteen with resources, the best strategy is to give them several options and have them choose their own. When preteens feel "forced" into a particular path, you can be sure they will run in the opposite direction!

Books
The Diary of Ann Frank, Ann Frank. This perennial classic has the power to inspire preteens through the power of the written word. Both boys and girls will benefit from the message of hope written here. (Fo)

Greater Than Angels, Carol Matas. Aladdin Paperbacks, 1999. (about $5). Tells of teenage holocaust survivors and the righteous gentiles who took them in. A wonderful look at the good in humankind. (Fr, Fo)

Jewish Sports Legends: The International Jewish Sports Hall of Fame, Joseph Siegman. Brasseys Inc., 1997. (about $30) Full of inspirational stories of sports greats from the past and present. (Fo, Fr)

Learning Torah : A Self-Guided Journey through the Layers of Jewish Learning, Joel Lurie Grishaver (illust.). UAHC Press, 1998. (about $10.00). A study guide for the Torah, including self-tests for motivated learners. (Fa)

The Midrash Says, Rabbi Moshe Weissman. B'nay Yakor Publications, 1988. (about $18). Separated by parsha, the volume includes explanations of customs and rituals that a fact-oriented child will enjoy. (Fa)

Menorahs, Mezuzas, and Other Jewish Symbols, Miriam Chaikin, illust. Erika Weihs. Clarion Books, 1990. (about $17). A great quick reference on a wide variety of Jewish symbols, nicely illustrated. Useful for younger readers also. (Fa)

Parallel Journeys, Eleanor H. Ayer, Helen Waterford, Alfons Heck. Atheneum, 1995. (about $16). The lives of a Hitler Youth member and teenage concentration camp survivor are described, looking at life before, during, and after the Shoah. A meeting 40 years after the Holocaust provides a strong message of common purpose. Based on true stories. (Fe, Fr)

Remarkable Jewish Women: Rebels, Rabbis, and Other Women from Biblical Times to the Present, Emily Taitz. Jewish Publication Society, 1996. (about $30). An inspiring collection of stories about Jewish women through the ages. A positive portrayal of the impact of Judaism on the lives of women from all walks of life. (Fo, Fa, Fr)

Shalom, Haver: Goodbye, Friend, Barbara Sofer. Kar-Ben Books, 1997. (about $17). Winner of an award for Jewish books, presents a moving and sensitive tribute to the late Yitzhak Rabin. (Fa, Fe, Fo)

Siddur (many versions). (from $20 to $50). Each child needs a siddur as soon as he or she can take care of one. Often available from synagogue gift shops, purchase one used in your temple's services. (All)

Tanakh-The Holy Scriptures, The Jewish Publication Society. Every son or daughter needs a Bible before they reach bar-bat mitzvah age. This is a must-have for every child. (All)

Tell It from the Torah, Gedalia Peterseil. Pitspopany Press, 1998. (about $25 for 2 volumes) A guide to the Torah with special sections on the holidays, including portions with Haftarah, discussion questions, and more. (Fa, Fo)

To Bigotry No Sanction: The Story of the Oldest Synagogue in America, Leonard Everett Fisher. Holiday House, 1999. (about $17). A tale of the religious history of early America, based on the Touro Synagogue of Newport, Rhode Island, oldest Jewish house of worship in the US. Includes photos and chronological index. (Fa, Fo)

Triumph of Survival—The Story of the Jews in the Modern Era (1650-1990), based on Rabbi Berel Wein's book, (about $60). This CD-Rom includes film clips, photographs, and audio to highlight the text. Also includes post 1990 information not found in the book. (Fa)

Youth Groups: At this critical age, connecting with other Jewish youth is important. Friendships and ideas created here can have a life-long impact. Each Jewish movement has its own organization and most have a preteen/junior high program:

Orthodox: National Conference of Synagogue Youth (NCSY) (212) 613-8233, www.ncsy.com

Conservative: United Synagogue Youth (USY) (212-533-7800), www.uscj.org/usy

Reform: National Federation of Temple Youth (NFTY) (914) 987-6300, www.rj.org/nfty

Internet Sources:
Sparks! (www.sparksmag.com) An online magazine with articles on current issues, movie reviews, and lots of Jewish content. (Fa)

Computer Games:
Jerusalem 3000—The CD-ROM. (about $50) An interactive encyclopedia that shows ancient and modern Jerusalem. Photos, animations, and games entice young teens to keep reading and learning. (Fa)

Teen Resources

Books: Teens are ready for adult-level reading material, but only in small doses. In general, they cannot handle a full-length book on any topic; reading a 10-page chapter is asking a great deal of the average teenager. The best books for this group are those that are divided into easy-reading chunks.

The Call of the Torah: An anthology of interpretation and commentary on the Five Books of Moses. Mesorah Publications, various prices. Five volumes comment of the weekly portions from each of the five books of Moses. A rich source of thought, and a springboard for further contemplation. (Fa)

The Jewish Book of Why, Alfred Kolatch. Jonathan David Publishers, 1981. (about $19). This now-classic book gives teens bite-size explanations on such topics as "why is a ninth candle used to light the others in the channukiah?", "why is hunting discouraged in the Jewish tradition?" as well as hundreds of others. (Fa)

Jewish Wisdom, Rabbi Joseph Telushkin. William Morrow, 1994. (about $25). This far-ranging collection of topics includes historical lessons on such far-ranging topics as truth-telling, tzedakah, human nature, and the holocaust. Each section is only a few pages, well within the allowable length for a teen's attention span. (Fo)

My Journal. Well, not exactly a book, but a reminder that journal-writing is a wonderful way to explore spirituality. Preteens and teens in this group find great comfort in keeping a daily log of their thoughts and feelings; buy one with an important-looking cover, and suggest they keep it somewhere private. (Fe)

One Thing I Ask: Riddles, Queries and Insights on the Siddur, Rabbi Hillel Fendel. Feldman Publishers, 1998. (about $15). This book, written in Q&A style, can serve as the basis for many games of "Jewish Trivia". The answers to many questions such as "what prayers do we recite once a year?", and "which of the Siddur's poems are based upon Maimonides' thirteen principles?" should keep them busy for quite some time. (Fa)

Pirke Avos: Ethics of the Fathers (Personal edition, 3 volume set). Mesorah Publications, 1996. (about $45). This classic text contains Jewish wisdom that has lasted centuries. The pocket edition contains rich explanations and anecdotes. (Fo)

The Search for Miri, Libby Lazewnik. Targum Press, 1991. (about $10). This story of self-discovery leads readers through a history of European Jewery and World War II. (Fr,Fo)

The Story of the Jews: A 4,000-year Adventure, Stan Mack. Villard Press, 1998. (about $20). A history book like you've never seen, made entirely in comic strip mode. Beginning with Abraham and ending with a family in space suits, this account tells history with a sense of humor. A must-see! (Fa)

Tanakh-The Holy Scriptures, The Jewish Publication Society. If your child doesn't have a Bible, provide one now. (All)

Traditions: The Complete Book of Prayers, Rituals and Blessings for Every Jewish Home, Sara Shendelman, Avram Davis. Hyperion, 1998. (about $22). Good explanations and great color photographs of all holidays and most practices. Written for adults, but teens will appreciate the amount of detail. (Fa)

Internet Sources
A Network for Jewish Youth (www.ort.org/anjy). Provided by the World ORT Union, the site includes a chat site, an on-line magazine, and an A-Z informational source on Jewish and Israeli issues (for all Jewish movements). (Fr)

Torah on the Information Superhighway (www.torah.org)

Sections on weekly portions, holiday observances, and more. (Fa)

Jewish Organizations

B'nai Brith Youth Organization (BBYO) For high-school students, a non-denominational group emphasizing social activities with a Jewish flavor. (Fr)

 C₰   C₰   C₰   C₰   C₰

10
"F" is for Family

Mother, Father, and God represent the core of the Jewish family life...Mother is there when you are ailing or hungry or cold, Father is always handy to protect you, and God is available for everything. (Dore Schary)

ભ   ભ   ભ   ભ   ભ

As most parents would agree, children don't seem to listen to what their elders say. "If I buy him a blue shirt, he wanted red. If I want to go to a movie, he wants to clean his room. I give up!" laments one parent. For many of us, getting our children to agree with us seems as hopeless as wanting grass to stop growing. Yet, we have mentioned before that *in the long run*, we parents have the greatest influence on who and what our children become. Think about your own experiences: how many times in a week do you say to yourself "I sound just like my mother!", or ask yourself what your own parents would do in a particular situation. Our children will have the same experiences when they are grown; what we do today has long-lasting repercussions.

On the negative side, we know that children who are abused become abusers, and neglected children develop poor interpersonal skills. In addition, adults who are prone to depression are more likely to have had parents who were detached and cold[10]. It stands to reason, then, that *positive* parenting would have positive effects on our children. This assumption is certainly true: research tells us that parents who are caring and involved create children with high self-esteem[11], and those who show warmth and love cause their children to value curiosity and intellectual growth[12].

Besides these positive effects, parents also have other, more subtle influences. Parents and families indirectly influence almost everything in a child's life from birth to young adulthood (don't tell them...they like to believe they're making their own choices). When families choose a first neighborhood, they pre-select the families for the child's early friendships. The schools they attend affect choices of friendships and feelings about education. When adults make decisions about television, movies, and videos, they are also deciding what will impact the child's view of the world. The bottom line is that families cannot avoid influencing their child's growth at every age.

Even in the teen years parents remain a critical factor, giving suggestions on important decisions such as college choices and career options. Teens pay considerable attention to their parents as role models; if both parents work, then that is the lifestyle chosen by their children. Parents of teens are shaking your heads at this point—it certainly seems as though teens ignore their parents for the most part. But they pay more attention to us that we realize; if they didn't pay attention to our habits, how could they sneak into the kitchen and grab an extra portion of ice cream, or listen to a forbidden program on the radio? We know that parents who feel that education is important create the same values in their children. And, parents who value Judaism and spirituality have children who do as well.

Our interviews brought up many examples of parents influencing their children's attitudes towards religion. When our research participants (Jewish, Christian, and even Buddhists) described the event that was most important in forming their ideas about religion and spirituality, they described times with friends, parents and grandparents. Here are some of the responses:

"When my mother and I prayed together at night...Praying with her was a positive experience because I still pray once in a while."

"I remember most going to church and seeing all my friends and family dressed up and happy. My parents were very involved in religion and I was taught the importance of faith."

"I began to realize that my family was happy 'cause we brought our problems to God...We believed that God was always there when we need him."

And then on the other side...
"...the main reason for my lack of strong religious belief is my parents. My parents aren't very religious, and their lack of religion influenced me."

It's clear that we pass some very basic feelings about religion to our children; we teach them volumes just by our actions. When we experience the richness of Judaism, we want with our whole hearts to give this gift to our children. As we have seen, families are absolutely capable of doing just that.

Judaism On Parents And Parenting

The Hebrew word for parents, *horim,* means guiding. True to that ideal of parenthood, the Jewish tradition has much to say about how a parent's guidance should be provided:

"A man should never single out one of his children for favored treatment, for because of two extra coins' worth of silk, which Jacob gave to Joseph and not to his other sons, Joseph's brothers became jealous of him, and one thing led to another until our ancestors became slaves in Egypt." Babylonian Talmud, Shabbat 10b.

"One should not promise a child something, and then not give it to him, because as a result, the child will learn to lie." Babylonian Talmud, Sukkah 46b.

"If you truly wish your children to study Torah, study it yourself in their presence. The will follow your example. Otherwise, they will not themselves study Torah but will simply instruct their children to do so." Rabbi Menahem Mendel of Kotzk

"And you shall love the Lord your God, with all you heart, with all your soul and with all your might. And these words which I command you this day, teach them to your children and talk about them..." Deuteronomy 6:5-6

And the results of that guidance:

"The best security for old age: respect your children." Sholem Asch

"What the child says in the street is the father's words, or the mother's." Sukkah, 56b.

Judaism offers more direction as well: we are to be concerned always for our children's welfare, even when they are grown[13]; parents should avoid creating fear in their children[14]; and we should teach our children to be honest in their affairs[15]. We are told that these tasks take precedence over our own comfort, our own needs.

Private Times: Between Parent and Child

The time that a parent or caregiver can be alone with a child are quite precious. In our rushed society, these special times can be few and far between. We adults are always rushing to pick up a child from lessons, get back from the store before sundown, or get all tasks accomplished before a spouse returns. Children are rushed to get their homework done, get to practice on time, or finish their chores before their favorite TV program. Private times are to be cherished , and create very special opportunities to form strong bonds. Like my recollection of gardening with my mother, these special times create long-lasting memories that have positive associations.

Private times are a chance to personalize your messages about Judaism and spirituality. When one parent and one child are together, a special magic occurs that binds heart to heart. Rabbi Schneerson has said, "Just as it is a mitzvah to put on *t'fillin* every day, it is a mitzvah for the father to be involved with the children every day."   Fathers and mothers both have a special responsibility to be with their children, to find time to link hearts and share life's important lesson. Some personal times are:

- Bath and bedtime rituals

- Picking up a child from lessons

- Walking with your child to a bus stop or to school

You can create other personal times as well by taking one child shopping with you, creating a special night once a week, or watching a television show together away from the rest of the family. Use these times to talk about Jewish ideas or values; the connection of this positive feeling and Judaism creates a powerful link with our Jewish heritage.

Family Times: Collective Judaism

It is said that one cannot be totally Jewish without being part of a group of Jews. The best way to begin is with the family—an "instant group" with love and encouragement already provided. There is a special synergy created in a group, especially when that group is the family; the energy level increases exponentially.

There are literally hundreds of ways families can show the importance of Judaism to their children. Whether one-on-one or with the entire family, activities that involve both adults *and* children are perhaps the most important ways to create interest in things Jewish. When parents, grandparents, aunts and uncles spend time on Jewish activities, their actions send a powerful message to children: this is important! Here are some ideas you can adapt for your own family:

Craft Projects: Creating a personal piece of Judaica is a fun experience, and can add an important dimension to faith if done as a family. Using wood, paper, fabric, or any other medium imaginable, wonderful pieces of family history can be produced. These projects can be individual or group projects, for personal use or to give as gifts, and can range from extremely home-spun to very professional in appearance. They can also be Jewish objects or "regular" objects with a Jewish look. Among the many examples of these projects are:

- A home-made *tzedakah* box (of wood, clay, or even a soup can). It has the further benefit of encouraging the giving of tzedakah.

- *Challah* covers (of felt or cloth). Shabbat is more special if personal creations cover the *challah*. Make several to give as gifts.

- School supplies. Jewish wrapping paper used as book covers, or binders decorated with Jewish symbols create a piece of Judaica that goes with your child every day.

- *Mezuzah* covers (of clay, wood, needlework). Your child can create a mezuzah for their room and hang it as part of a family celebration.

- Wrapping paper (rubber stamps, paints, stickers). How much more fun to wrap a birthday or Chanukah gift in your own creation!

- *Kiddush* cup or *Seder* plate. The new paint-your-own ceramics stores make it possible to create many items for special occasions. How about creating your own Passover tableware?

- Home-made *Hanukkah* gifts. Instead of store-bought gifts, consider making treats for your family members instead.

Judaica in the Home: A critical way to show pride in your Jewish heritage is to display it in your home. There are possibilities for every room in the house, and Judaism becomes part of everyday life when we see reminders of it everywhere. In his book "40 Things You Can Do to Save the Jewish People", Joel Grishaver suggests having your children give *you* a tour of the Judaica in your home. Make them learn the history of each purchase or gift as well its purpose in Jewish life. Being a family "docent" will make them more appreciative of your family's history and satisfy all four aspects: for the Fact-focused there is information, Feeling children can hear positive stories, those who emphasize Friends create an attachment to their past, and the Focus-based group learns more about ritual objects and their use.

- Jewish art. Each Jewish home can have some artwork with a Jewish content. Ranging from masterpieces to framed $3.50 cards, art with Jewish themes can be found to fit any taste, style, or color scheme.

- *Mezuzot.* Each interior room, aside from bathrooms, can have a *mezuzah.* These special symbols of the Jewish faith serve as a constant reminder that God is with us as we go through our day.

- Ritual objects. Consider displaying your *Seder* plate, Shabbat candlesticks, or special *dreidl* all year. Having reminders of special days always visible enriches the ties to Judaism in children *and* adults.

- Jewish books. There are history books, prayer books, story books and more that can create reminders of Judaism. These books can be placed on a special shelf, or distributed around the house. One family places a Jewish book in each room as a reminder that there is always something more to learn about God.

- Music. Playing Jewish music puts a special feeling in the air. If your family members are lucky enough to play instruments, a monthly Jewish concert can be a positive experience.

Shabbat Celebrations: Observing Shabbat together as a family is perhaps the best way to create a connection between Judaism and your children. Shabbat is a gift from God to the Jews that creates a break from the rest of the week. Sharing this special time, even in small ways, shows children the unique place God has for the Jewish people. Some ideas for sharing Shabbat with the family are listed here:

- Shabbat meals. It comes naturally to some families to prepare a Shabbat meal on Friday night, lighting the Shabbat candles and giving thanks to God for taking us through another week. For others, it is more difficult to come home from a long day of work and "turn off everything" for several hours. Sharing a Shabbat dinner, from *Kiddush* to *Birkhat Ha-Mazon* (grace after meals) can show children an important example about the special nature of Shabbat.

- Go for a walk or hike together. Get the family out for a walk, short or long, where you can experience a bit of nature.

- Take a nap. It's traditional to take naps on Shabbat afternoon, showing that you honor the commandment to rest on that day.

- Study together. Choose a short passage from Torah and talk to your children about how it applies to you. Jewish calendars normally have the weekly Torah portion listed each Shabbat; take out your *Tanakh* and learn together.

- Sing and play games. Singing on Shabbat is said to be a mitzvah, for it brings down God's blessings. Playing games together as a family is fun for all, and creates a special positive feeling.

Family discussions: In most families, discussions have more impact if they arise spontaneously. The exception to this rule occurs if parents AND children are attracted to the aspect of intellect (Fact); in this case, your child will appreciate a regular time each week devoted to learning and family discussions. One difficulty that parents have is in making these times a *discussion*, rather than a lecture. A helpful tip is to begin by asking your child's opinion, and then provide gentle correction where their ideas or facts may be wrong. There are many events that can begin meaningful discussions; some of the most obvious are:

- Movies. There are many movies with Jewish themes, either current releases or on video. Stop for an ice cream or for dinner afterwards and listen to what your children have to say.

- News events. With any big news event, there is a Jewish value or similar time in history that can be discussed. Linking Judaism to news stories shows faith's relevance to daily life.

- School and neighborhood events. Did your neighbor's dog bark all night? Did someone cheat on a test? These events present a good opportunity to talk about Jewish ideas such as *Derech eretz* (common decency) and honesty.

Group Study: When parents or grandparents study *with* children, learning becomes something valuable. There are many areas of study and types of materials; some are listed below:

- Weekly Torah portion (*parsha*). Each week of the Hebrew calendar has an assigned portion so the Torah can be read beginning to end each year. There are many excellent commentaries that can be the beginnings of some important family discussions.

- Jewish history. We often need to know where we have been before we can see where we are going. It can be fun to look at a map of the Middle East together, tracing the paths of some important Jewish events.

- Child as teacher. Help a child research a question, such as "when was Purim first celebrated", to teach to the rest of the family.

Holiday celebrations: Another excellent way to

create a lasting link to Judaism is to create home holiday celebrations. Because of the natural positive feelings in families, holidays at home become important remembrances that can tie a child closely to his or her Jewish heritage. These celebrations have value for each of the four faith benefits:

- Customs and rituals (Focus). Create holiday customs to repeat each year, giving children a sense of continuity. The "same time next year" qualities of family customs satisfy the common question of the aspect of guidance: "how do we do this?"

- Opportunities to learn (Facts). It seems there are always new and interesting facts to learn about holy days and festivals. Provide interesting "tidbits" for your fact-focused children, or let them teach *you*, to spark their interest anew each year.

- Group celebrations (Friends). Just the fact that your celebrations involve many people is good enough to satisfy the search for relationship. If your family consists of only yourself and your child, consider joining with another family to add variety to your celebrations.

- Warmth and happiness (Feelings). Celebrating with others we care for is all about "warm fuzzies". These feelings of comfort and satisfaction satisfy the aspect of emotion each time a holiday comes.

Family Projects: Choose a way for your family to actively support Jewish principles. Whether you label it "social action" or *tikkun olam*, Judaism has always stood for bringing Jewish values into real-world situations. There are many ways to practice this idea:

- *Tzedakah* projects. Begin a short-term project such as collecting canned goods for a local food pantry.

- Volunteer your time. There are many charities, Jewish and non-Jewish, that can use help. Find one that interests your family and make a commitment for six months of volunteer hours.

- Give *tzedakah*. Children need to learn the value of giving money. Provide a *pushkah* and have everyone empty their pockets each Shabbat.

More ideas

There are hundreds of other ideas that can bring a sense of spirituality into our everyday family life. Look through the following suggestions for ideas you can use with a single child or the whole family. Many will be of interest to a particular group; they are marked with the short-hand version of the group's name (Fa, Fe, Fr, Fo).

- Teach your child a short meditation. There are many excellent resources available, and a five-minute break from the regular hassles of life will be good for you both. (Fe)

- Create a sacred spot in your home or child's bedroom. Include pictures of special people or objects from significant places or events. (Fe)

- Comment on acts of kindness during the day. Everyone can use encouragement and validation that they are learning the right ways.

- Visit an empty sanctuary. There is a special feeling that fills the air in sacred spaces; allow your child to feel the presence of God.

- Write a family blessing. Judaism encourages blessings for special events—and even finishing homework or playing a good quarter of soccer can qualify! In Hebrew or English, a special blessing makes Judaism a part of everyday life.

- Send a card to someone each week/month. What a nice way to practice lovingkindness—especially if the card is just to say "hello". (Fr)

- Walk silently in nature. Go to a park and experience birds singing, flowers smelling, wind blowing. God's presence is everywhere. (Fe)

- Read about other religious traditions. Discuss the similar values (being kind, for example) and holidays (Passover and Easter). (Fa, Fo)

- Stage a puppet show or play. Help your children create their own production using a religious theme. (Fo, Fr)

- Create a "You Are Special" day. At dinner once a week, one person gets a special plate. The rest of the family all mention positive things about that person.

- Write stories about God. Have your child describe what s/he thinks God is like (nothing is wrong!) (Fe)

- Perform random acts of kindness. As a family, help someone in need or give away something that is missing. You will all feel good afterwards!

- Create a family "clear the air" ritual. Declare a time when guilt, angry feelings or sadnesses can be burned like *chametz* or cast to the fish as in *Tashlikh*. (Fo, Fe)

- Create a family "amen". Find a special way that your family can finish prayers. Some families use a single hand clap, others have a special melody. Be creative!

- Change the words to a common melody for Shabbat, Passover, or *Hanukkah*. Pre-teens can be very creative with words; let them write a personal verse or two for *Lecha Dodi* or Dreidl, Dreidl (Fo, Fe)

- Have older children teach younger ones prayers or songs, or explain the holidays to young cousins.

- Invite teens to lead parts of the Passover Seder. Many segments are actually fun to read, and can involve them in a positive way.

Among these ideas are many suggestions your family can use. As you look for the right choices for your family, keep in mind (1) your children's primary factors, (2) *your* interests, and (3) a sense of balance. It is critical to introduce children to all four faith benefits, so be sure that your choices cover all four needs. Remember that each activity can meet many needs. For example, many children will stay involved in a teaching or fact-based activity with their parents or grandparents just because they want to be with you (a Feeling or Friends focus). As you cycle through the holidays each year, find a different family activity that meets one of the four needs—the need for information, comfort, relationship, or guidance.

This chapter has included the not-so-subtle insistence that *parents and grandparents* need to be as involved with their faith as they want their child to be. To rephrase the common statement, "an action is worth a thousand words". *You* are the best resource for your children; family members have the longest-lasting influence and the greatest chance of creating spirituality in children. Involve him or her in as many Jewish acts as you can; allow them to listen while you pray, to watch while *t'fillin* is laid, and help with *challah* baking.

For some of us this task is difficult. We have not been as involved with our faith as we would like, and we don't quite know where to begin being an example. The good news is that these four faith benefits are as relevant for adults as they are for children. In Part Three, you will find help to discover your own primary factor and find many ways to grow adult faith. What a strong example that shows your child! When children see our own desire to grow in faith, it creates in them an equal appetite to build their Jewish background as well.

ೞ   ೞ   ೞ   ೞ   ೞ

11
The Faith Profiler:
Growing Adult Faith

CB   CB   CB   CB   CB

There are countless resources and ideas to increase your child's ties to faith, but the best way of all to create a bond between your child and Judaism is to provide a committed, long-term model for them to follow. Children generally don't become more observant or more spiritual than their parents or families—we set the bar which becomes their goal. As we have said before, this commitment begins early and lasts long, even into the college years. In spite of parental concerns that college life may make their child *less* interested in spiritual matters, it appears that the stresses of college life may in fact turn students towards their faith...*if* religion was a significant part of their formative years. The majority of college students in our studies said that the main reason they remained involved with religion was because of their family's involvement with faith.

For these reasons, parents (and grandparents) should think seriously about their own involvement in Judaism. Each of us can enrich our own spirituality using the same faith factors we have described for our children. One of the four paths of Fact, Feeling, Friends or Focus will come to us more naturally; it is here that we should focus our own growth. But before beginning

147

that process, let's examine some of the issues that affect the growth of adult faith. For most of us the path to faith is not a straight one; it's a road that sometimes becomes overgrown and seemingly impossible to travel.

> *Life is what happens while we're making other*
> *plans. (Anonymous)*

ଓଃ   ଓଃ   ଓଃ   ଓଃ   ଓଃ

One of faith's miracles is Judaism is complex enough to serve us in many different ways. As we adjust to the various challenges of living, different facets of the jewel that is our faith will shine forth. Although one path will likely always be our preferred avenue, the other three aspects of faith will come into focus at various times, depending upon our life stage or the current issues we face. A mother with preschool children may feel a need for social involvement with other families, and will turn to the aspect of Friends to connect with her faith. When the children become involved in sports teams and she joins the PTA, there may be little time for other social involvements and she may turn instead to the aspect of Focus as she shows her children how to weave Judaism into daily life. When the children enter the teen years she may feel drawn to the intellectual side of faith (Facts) as sons and daughters begin to ask probing questions. Even later, when she becomes a senior citizen, she may be drawn back again to Friends as her social networks become entwined with other families in the congregation. Likewise, the demands of a career may create similar tugs and pulls over the years.

Our needs change as an inevitable part of life, but changes often occurs so slowly we don't even notice it happening. We may be pulled away from religious involvement because of time commitments, work deadlines and the like. Sometimes we simply drift away from our congregational ties, ending up with no connection to religion and no desire to expand

148

as a spiritual being. Other times, we may decide that we need faith of another flavor. We search for a group of people with whom we identify, and we decide to follow another religion that holds more excitement for us. While it is true that *congregations* can sometimes cease to meet our needs, it would be a fallacy to assume that in all of Judaism there is nothing to fulfill our new desires. Judaism has been around for centuries precisely *because* it can appeal to people of all types, ages, and situations. As with all faiths, there is great personal value to be discovered in Judaism, but sometimes work is required to clear the path. Regardless of whether we have a strong grip or the tiniest toe-hold on faith, we can still benefit from Judaism's ability to interpret life, comfort us, guide us and connect us to others.

Preferences of other household members also impact our paths to faith. In one family I interviewed, the wife was extremely interested in the intellectual side of her faith. Her husband was more interested in the social connections, but he came to Torah studies anyway to be with his wife, and ended up becoming friends with another man in the study group. Following his wife's desires, he also accomplished his own goal for fellowship and connection. Rarely does a particular activity meet only one need; exploring new options can sometimes reap unexpected rewards.

Determining your faith aspect

You may already know, from description in earlier chapters, which of the four aspects of faith is your highest priority. But if your primary path is not clear to you, a "roadmap" is provided to help you along. Immediately following is a 40-question Faith Profiler that will help you find the aspect that you (or your spouse) gravitate towards naturally. Questions and scoring for the Faith Profiler were confirmed in several studies at the University of California, Irvine. For each of the statements, simply decide whether you agree or disagree, and how strongly. When you have finished all forty questions, follow the easy scoring guide to create a personal profile.

Adult Faith Profiler

On the line in front of each questions, put a number from 1-4:

1 = Strongly Disagree
2 = Mostly Disagree
3 = Mostly Agree
4 = Strongly Agree

____ 1. My faith clears up all of life's mysteries.

____ 2. It is important to belong to a group of believers.

____ 3. I gain tremendous peace and comfort from my spirituality.

____ 4. The best way to direct your life is to base it on spiritual ideas.

____ 5. The teachings of my religion are fascinating.

____ 6. Belonging to a spiritual community is very important.

____ 7. Because of my religion, I have a strong sense of being cared for.

____ 8. All of the foundations for daily living are found in religious teachings.

____ 9. I enjoy understanding important religious issues more than most other people.

____ 10. I enjoy talking about my religion with others who share my faith.

____ 11. Receiving answers to prayers gives me a strong sense of comfort.

____ 12. Religion and spirituality create the best basis for daily life.

____ 13. When I find a religious issue I don't understand, I explore it until it's clear.

____ 14. Sharing your faith in a religious community is very important.

_____ 15. My spirituality makes me feel loved.

_____ 16. I try very hard to emphasize religious ideals.

_____ 17. I understand the teaching of my religious tradition completely.

_____ 18. Being connected to others in your congregation is a key part of spirituality.

_____ 19. Religion/spirituality gives me a strong sense of peace.

_____ 20. If a problem can be solved with religious ideals, that is the best solution.

_____ 21. Having discussions of spiritual issues is fun for me.

_____ 22. Celebrating faith as part of a religious community is truly rewarding.

_____ 23. When I think of religion, I think of endless love.

_____ 24. My daily life is focused on religious ideals.

_____ 25. My faith gives me a thorough understanding of why things happen.

_____ 26. Connecting with others by performing religious rituals is truly rewarding.

_____ 27. I feel a strong sense of connection to God.

_____ 28. I can only understand life if I think in religious terms.

_____ 29. Understanding the purpose of life is a religious/spiritual issue.

_____ 30. Knowing that others are worshipping just as you are is very comforting.

_____ 31. Spirituality or religion always makes a person stronger.

_____ 32. Spiritual ideals should be used in deciding how to treat other people.

_____ 33. I often look for chances to learn more about spiritual issues.

_____ 34. Being with others in a religious community always brings me closer to God.

_____ 35. Comfort and peace are always the end result of being spiritual.

_____ 36. Religion tells people how to deal with every-day decisions.

_____ 37. Religious/spiritual teachings give me an understanding

of life's purpose.
____ 38. Joining with others to share our faith is a very positive
experience.
____ 39. Religious people are peaceful people.
____ 40. I know how to treat other people because of my religious
background.

Faith Profile Scoring Key

Fact—Add scores for questions 1, 5, 9, 13, 17, 21, 25, 29, 33, 37
Total score for FACT _____

Feelings—Add scores for 2, 6, 10, 14, 18, 22, 26, 30, 34, 38
Total score for FEELINGS _____

Friends—Add scores for 3, 7, 11, 15, 19, 23, 27, 31, 35, 39
Total score for FRIENDS _____

Focus—Add scores for 4, 8, 12, 16, 20, 24, 28, 32, 36, 40
Total score for FOCUS _____

The aspect with the largest total is your natural
inclination—your prevalent aspect. It is common to have a
second aspect whose point total is close to your primary factor;
you will find personal value in exploring this aspect as well.

Each of the four following chapters will help you
understand a particular faith emphasis. As with faith in children,
each of the aspects creates one wall of the house of faith. A
complete house of worship is composed of four walls—intellect,
emotions, desire for connection, and a need for guidance are all
essential to build a strong foundation in faith. As you help your
children our grandchildren enhance their own faith, take
advantage of the activities you plan for them even if your child's
chosen aspect is different from your own.

12

The Search For Understanding: The Path Of Intellect

To be conscious that you are ignorant is a great step to knowledge. (Benjamin Disraeli)

ଔ   ଔ   ଔ   ଔ   ଔ

Don is a 56-year-old acoustical engineer, and an active participant his synagogue's weekly Torah study class. After study on Shabbat morning the members meet at a local coffee shop for lunch. As they wait for their sandwiches to arrive, Don will ask the group's opinion on some obscure piece of knowledge based on the Biblical reading for the week. Usually, no one but Don much cares about the issue, let alone has an opinion one way or another. But he explains his logic with such elegance that everyone sits mesmerized, listening to his stories right through lunch. Besides the group in his own congregation, Don attends at least two other groups each week. He loves the interaction and the learning he receives. Don's faith is tied to the path of intellect: he is in a constant search for understanding and information.

The search for meaning is a hallmark of this path to faith. There is always something more to be learned, something further to be explored. It seems as though seeking knowledge is more important than obtaining it; if there is an end to the quest, it is not in this lifetime.

Major Emphasis

Most of those following the path of Fact read voraciously, and have extensive religious libraries that cause spouses to roll their eyes. Bookstores have an irresistible pull on them, and they seldom leave without a parcel—large or small— under their arm. Many of them also enjoy debating points of doctrine ad infinitum. It seems as though every chance meeting with a friend is a time to re-discover some morsel of wisdom. In short, those of us enmeshed in the Aspect of Intellect crave information.

In this continuous search for data and facts, three major "quests" can be distinguished. The first and most fundamental goal, expressed unanimously by these folks, is a search for answers to life's questions. Almost all of those interviewed were looking to find out "why am I here?" Darla, Jewish and a mother of three, says that when she prays "(I get) a sense of purpose, re-clarification: 'oh yah, okay, that's what it's about' ". Yet another woman said that in her spiritual search, "I become aware of something that I didn't see before—a message that suddenly becomes visible." For followers of this aspect, faith becomes a way to find answers.

The second important issue of this faith factor is gaining a new perspective—thinking about issues in a new way. Using the path of Fact the powers of thought are sharpened by attempting to make connections that were not apparent before. Says one person, "If it's really good preaching, it sets you thinking." It is this challenge that excites the "fact-seeker" above all.

It is often true that the *search* for answers is more important than the answers themselves. On the way to understanding one issue, there is always the exciting opportunity to become side-tracked solving yet another mystery[16]. Whereas others are frustrated by obtuse passages and conflicting evidence, those pursuing Fact seem to plunge in with both feet, looking for clues and thriving on every piece of new information that presents itself. The intricacies and seeming contradictions in sacred writings are of great interest, for they represent mysteries to be unraveled.

The power of this faith factor comes from the insistence that every seeming contradiction *can* in fact be explained; that every question of life *does* have an answer that can be found through diligent study, reflection, and discussion. It is this strong belief in the power of the human mind that convinces those pursuing the aspect of intellect to continue their search for knowledge.

A third goal for those on this path is to find the lesson behind events in our lives. Tanya, a Catholic in her 30's, greets her coworkers regularly with "Do you know what happened to me last night?" She then recounts a common event, perhaps her cat stayed out all night which caused her to worry about its safety. She generally concludes with the statement "And so, I learned that God has a hand in everything." In the simplest of occurrences, Tanya seeks for the "lesson" that is there waiting for her, and generally finds one. She uses the aspect of intellect without looking in books or talking to others; she simply looks inward for guidance.

Internal & External Aspects

In adults, each aspect of faith has two versions—an outward and an inward orientation. Depending mostly on personality traits, each individual will choose an outward/extroverted way of dealing with intellectual questions or an inward/introverted perspective. The *outward* path of Fact shows itself in a desire for discussion, argumentation, and philosophical exchange; the *inward* orientation looks to books and personal contemplation for answers.

Looking outward: Consider Michael, a 48-year-old self-employed computer consultant from Pittsburgh. Each time he greets his friends, he launches into a monologue beginning with "I got a new one for ya…" He then continues to describe, in detail, a hypothetical situation involving some dilemma to be resolved using biblical standards. He usually concludes with "So, what do you think the Bible says about that?" Regardless of your response, you are deluged with a lengthy discussion on the inconsistencies and exceptions that Michael has thought through previously. Michael enjoys exercising the external factor of Fact, which involves discussion and debate on issues of biblical interpretation, application of spiritual principles, and differences in religious traditions. He looks for input from others to help him make decisions on spiritual matters. Externalizers need the stimulation of others to be able to exercise their full intellectual power, and often seek out study groups and open forums for the discussion of religious issues.

Looking inward: Others prefer a more private route to understanding. The *internal* aspect expresses itself in reading, journaling, and other solitary pursuits of knowledge. Those pursuing this internal emphasis have large libraries, join reading groups and book clubs, and often listen to religious programming on radio or television as ways to gather information. While they most certainly discuss their ideas with others, they generally do so *after* forming their own opinions from the information they have gathered.

Fundamental Truth Of Intellect

As with each of the Aspects, a common thread was woven through each person's discussion of the search for understanding. For Fact, the aspect of intellect, the theme is that ***God grants understanding.*** Truth is out there, and is easily found when one looks through the glasses of faith. Whether the search is for personal answers or esoteric reality, those who pursue Fact are confident that understanding can be obtained through the path of faith and spirituality. Answers to major *and* minor questions are available to everyone who truly cares to seek the truth.

Once wisdom has entered your heart
And knowledge is sweet to your soul,
Reflection shall watch over you
To deliver you from the way of evil,
From any man who speaks perversely.
(Proverbs 2:11-12)

ଔ   ଔ   ଔ   ଔ   ଔ

Most Rewarding Activities

Study groups: Both internalizers and externalizers enjoy the stimulation of listening to the ideas of others. The externalizing group leans toward debate and lengthy discussion. Those with an inward leaning enjoy study groups as well, and may simply listen to others and process the facts themselves. Still, study groups provide both types with that which they crave—ideas and information. Michael, our friend with all the questions, regularly changes congregational affiliation because "the people aren't stimulating any more". He likes to join study groups, and will stick with a group for a year or two until he has heard all that the members have to say. Then he'll move on, hoping for new ideas and new information.

Sermons and talks: For those pursuing the Aspect of Intellect, the best part of the religious service is usually the *D'var Torah*, the rabbi's message. As one gentleman mentioned, "I like something to think about for the rest of the week." When Fact-oriented adults choose a new congregation, the most important factor is likely to be the depth of content in the weekly message; more is definitely better.

Workshops: Specialized workshops, where half a day is spent exploring a single topic, are always welcomed by this group. Often the topic of the seminar is a side issue; if the seminar leader is an expert in the field or there is a promise of extensive hand-outs, you can bet that most adults following this path will put it on their calendar.

Talmud study: Studying the reasons and justifications for Jewish beliefs and practices can be an exciting endeavor. "Fact-seekers" find great fulfillment in understanding the foundations of one's faith and following the logical trail to its current practice.

Internet resources: The WorldWide Web has exploded with information on religion. The internet contains official homepages for every major religious tradition, and many small belief systems as well. The Internet has become a place of instant information, and a very exciting resource for those seeking religious facts. A certain psychology/religion professor-turned- author, who shall remain nameless, has (at last count) six three-ring binders full of webpage printouts from religious websites in her office. Electronic bulletin boards and list-serves provide ways to interact with distant others, providing even more information and "food for thought".

Fact in Example

The path of intellect, Fact, is put to use each time we study scripture. When we try to teach our children the meaning of words, phrases, or passages, we appeal to their intellect to grasp the information. We use the path of Fact whenever we struggle to understand the essence of a Torah passage. And it is Fact, our ability to reason, that links each small piece of data to the larger whole. Through reason we reveal the intricate pattern of our personal theology and find the underlying theme in our faith. Without intellect to piece our ideas together, we have only disconnected bits of information and sound-bites of Judaism.

The world of religion is full of seekers after truth who model the aspect of intellect. One of the earliest examples is Rashi (*R*abbi *Sh*lomo *I*tzhaki), an 11th century scholar. He manufactured wine in Northern France for his livelihood, and from the clarity of his writings it is obvious that he did not over-indulge in his product! He wrote a massive commentary on both the Torah and the Talmud, receiving acclaim for his unique ability to examine each word and each grammatical nuance for meaning. The extent of his commentary has not been duplicated by anyone. The depth of thought expressed in his writings exemplifies Fact, showing intellect at its very best.

In more modern times, several current authors demonstrate the depth of ideas possible using the path of Fact. Mordecai Kaplan, writing in the 1930s, clearly explained with great lucidity why none of the existing religious movements were capable of providing support to diaspora Jews in a modern age. His convinc-ing arguments led to the birth of the Reconstructionist movement. Dennis Prager, a noted speaker, author, and talk-show host, is most known for his in-depth and thoughtful analysis of ethical and religious questions. Both of these men display Fact in their reasoned justifications for their heart-felt positions.

Practices to Expand this Aspect

There are many ways to enhance the Fact perspective with fulfilling activities and resources. Here are fifteen living examples, as suggested by people oriented toward the path of Fact.

1. *Join a religious book club.* Most clubs offer a monthly selection, and having a new viewpoint or idea delivered to your door regularly is an exciting prospect.

2. *Listen to the viewpoint of someone outside of your own denomination.* Expose yourself to different viewpoints to help you to understanding our own convictions. Contrary to common lore, listening to different ideas most often *strengthens* our own ideas rather than weakening them.

3. *Become part of an Internet discussion group, or start one of your own.* Most bulletin boards have several discussions going on at once; it is fast and easy to begin a discussion, add your own ideas, or look at other people's ideas on a particular topic.

4. *Start a journal of your thoughts.* Keep track of your progress towards understanding. This practice can be extremely rewarding; some people look back over their previous writings before praying or meditating.

5. *Look up some traditional prayers and learn their origins.* Uncover the history of a particular piece of religious literature and provide insight into our own questions. Knowing why we stand while reciting the *Amida* prayer, for example, enriches our own prayer practice.

6. *Attend services on a regular basis, and make a list of the*

sermon topics. Document what your rabbi or guest speakers discuss during the year. Create an annual list than will give you an understanding of the congregation's values. (What topics are discussed regularly; what topics are only discussed in passing; which subjects are brought up again after services are concluded?)

7. Read religious history to discover the issues that were important in creating your denomination. Most denominations and movements began because of a disagreement about doctrine or religious activities. These "roots" can provide a solid basis for finding answers to current questions.

8. Discuss questions with the congregation's spiritual leaders. The views of learned men and women can be extremely valuable, providing direction to those looking for answers. Their points of view are extremely valuable in directing "seekers" in the proper direction.

9. Listen to the beliefs of others. Often we can learn valuable lessons and unravel complex puzzles merely by listening to what others have to say. Listen objectively, without asking questions, and create a valuable and rewarding experience.

10. Join a Torah study group. This suggestion is almost too obvious; find a group where discussion is encouraged and multiple viewpoints are welcomed.

11.Use the events of the day in your daily meditations or prayers. Look back over the day's happenings to provide "lessons" on life's purpose and your own spiritual path.

12. Read a book written by a well-known theologian or spiritual thinker. Thoughts that survive for decades or centuries are always based upon solid analysis and deep thought. When we can understand the points of others, we often clarify our own ideas.

13. Attend workshops on interesting spiritual topics. Workshops and speaker-series are great sources for information and networking, and can help "fill in the blanks" as we search for understanding.

14. Read the religion section in the newspaper. More than just a list of congregations, the religion section of most newspapers contains articles on current religious debates, biographies of individuals in the news, and other timely information.

15. Subscribe to Jewish publications. Each Jewish movement has an official newsletters, magazines, or other periodicals. These materials are an excellent source of current, relevant facts and knowledge—on a regular basis.)

Enriching The Journey

It takes a powerful mind to answer the important questions of life. Those who have the ability to understand complex truths are truly blessed and should seriously consider sharing their know-ledge with others. The study of Torah, an essential component of Judaism, begins with this path to faith.

Those who favor Fact need also to pay attention to the other three factors as well. When you join (or form) a learning-focused havurah, you combine the path of Fact with that of Friends. Likewise, teaching a course in Judaism compounds Fact with Focus. Finally, joining the paths of Fact and of Feelings leads to a more "grounded" approach to one's faith, where facts back up the feelings of love and safety. To continue your journey and add to your spiritual wealth, it is important to enhance your primary orientation with the other aspects of faith. A spiritual life is not limited to a single perspective.

> *The important thing is not to stop questioning.*
> *(Albert Einstein)*

      ೞ   ೞ   ೞ   ೞ   ೞ

13
Feelings—Looking for Peace in All the Right Places

When the heart is full, the eyes overflow. (Yiddish folksaying)

ଓଃ   ଓଃ   ଓଃ   ଓଃ   ଓଃ

    Sarah is 35 and the mother of two children. For her, the main focus of her relationship with God is to find feelings of peace for herself. "Peace to accept whatever comes my way," she says, "any problems and...you know, having tragic things or (a) crisis, that I know I'll get through it, and I can handle it." Bob and Bert are both Jewish, and although they are separated by two decades in age and belong to two different Jewish movements, they both talk about feelings of "shalom" or peace as the main benefit of their Judaism. "Usually, prayer relaxes me,", says 62-year-old Bob. "I get an emotional charge for the rest of the day." Thirty-nine-year-old Bert also says that daily prayer leaves him with a "good warm feeling", and that he enjoys the Sabbath as the high point of his week. All three of these adults are describing the path of Feelings—looking for emotional fulfillment through faith.

    Feelings of comfort, peace and safety are common in

spirituality. But while most of us feel these emotions from time to time in our spiritual quest, those individuals following the path of Feelings *require* a bond of emotion to tie them to their faith. These seekers of peace long for an emotional connection to Judaism and thus to God, just as those on the path of Friends seek a connection in friendship with faithful others.

Major Emphasis

Emotions and feelings are an important part of "being human". To be called unemotional is usually an insult, and people question our psychological balance if we show the wrong emotional reaction to an important event. Emotion plays an important part in spirituality, as well. Two thirds of the adults interviewed for this project mentioned positive emotions in relation to religious events, the most common being peace, comfort, and a feeling of being loved.

The major emphasis of the aspect of Feeling is a focus on receiving an inner confirmation of personal spirituality. This faith factor provides internal affirmation of outward religious acts, either now or in the future. Some people feel peaceful and "enclosed by God's love" after attending religious services; still others focus on the future, describing a sense of comfort in knowing that they will be taken care of, either in life or after death. Sue, a Catholic in her 50's (remember that these aspects cross denominational boundaries), says after praying she feels comforted "just to know that He's listening. What I want I don't always get, but I know that He'll always do what's best for me."

Those of us who use this path to spirituality generally enjoy weekly services, and feel enriched by the music and prayers in which they participate. One identifying characteristic of this group is an enchantment with music—song's magical ability to touch souls resonates strongly with those pursuing the path of Feelings. Large collections of CDs and tapes are to be expected with this group; even music that is not religious in content can often invoke positive religious feelings. Another hallmark of this group is a marked *dis*interest in intellectual explanations. When discussing the reasons behind a particular custom or ritual, for example, the eyes of Feeling types usually glaze over, waiting until the end of the discussion to say "Well, it's always felt right to me, that's why I do it." No reasons or explanations are necessary; if it feels right, that's it.

While not a large group, those searching for Feelings are very specific in their needs. If they do not feel connected emotionally it is unlikely they will remain involved in their faith, as the need for an emotional link is their first priority. Besides religious services, this emotional satisfaction can come from unexpected places such as viewing a beautiful sunset, taking a walk in the woods, or seeing the success of a loved one. The emotional swell that most of us feel one these occasions turns into an experience of holiness for the Feelings person.

Feeling individuals are after one of three emotional rewards: feelings of comfort, feelings of peace, or feelings of safety. (And if *two* of these states can be achieved, even better!) Comfort is most often mentioned by those who were raised in the Catholic faith—teachings of the Roman Catholic church often involve the statement that God will take care of us. As one Catholic man stated, "there is a comfort in knowing one way or another that I am going to be taken care of." Peace also plays an important role for this group, especially as a benefit of going to weekly services. Feelings of shalom often last throughout the week, making Feeling-focused individuals look forward to the next Shabbat service where positive feelings can once again be renewed. For younger adults, the word most frequently used in describing emotional benefits is "safety" . Feeling safe and protected from life's problems ranks high on the list of positive feelings received by the Feelings group.

For some, the feelings emerging from faith have no adequate description. A general sense that "everything is OK" is all that can be said. In the words of one woman, "It's just a feeling that all is well." These words tell of the deep emotions that are tapped by spirituality; when one is on this path, all is right in the world.

Internal & External Aspects

As with all paths to faith, the path of Feelings has two ways of being expressed—an internal or inward-looking manifestation and an external or outward appearance. The external expression is easier to identify; it is always accompanied by an outward demonstration of emotion. Dancing, singing, and generally being carried away by the emotions of the moment are all clear signs of an externally-focused Feeling person. It is easy to find these individuals on Purim, for example, when dancing is encouraged. These folks generally lead the dancing, and seem the most comfortable in this setting. In some Christian settings, upraised hands and loud prayer denote these individuals. After a moving concert, these are the individuals with tears in their eyes or blissful smiles on their faces, announcing their intense involvement with the music.

Internal Feeling types, on the contrary, can be identified by their silence and to some extent by their *lack* of response. For these people, emotion is a very personal thing and not to be shared with any but the closest of friends or family (and frequently not shared at all). Those of us in this category can be quite moved, but all the movement is an internal emotional churning that defies expression. It is almost as if putting words to the feeling negates the emotions altogether. This group of faith seekers, although small, perhaps has the most intense tie to spirituality of any group, for it seems that their very being is involved in their faith. It is not coincidental that this group produces poets and musicians; their intense emotional feelings are best expressed in metaphor and song.

Fundamental Truth Of Feelings

Each aspect has a fundamental theme that is woven as a common thread through numerous individual stories. For the aspect of emotion, that theme is *God fulfills.* Each of us has an empty place inside that yearns for completion. When that space is fill with love, comfort and peace from God, it pulls us back again and again. Once we experience being filled by God we are compelled to return to God for the same rich reward; nothing else can replace it.

Most Rewarding Activities

"Mystical" elements of the faith: The teachings of Kabbalah, the Jewish mystical tradition, involve touching the ultimate in a way that is beyond reason or the senses. These mystical teachings are usually of great interest to individuals who are engaged in the inward exploration of connection: connecting with God. Mystical traditions promise a way to communicate or connect more directly with the infinite, and to understand God's wishes more fully. Taken to its farthest extent, mysticism claims to bring us to a place where the greatest degree of understanding or power is possible—more than is otherwise accessible to humankind[17]. In its striving for a strong connection to God or universal truth, mysticism becomes an important pathway for those seeking this relationship.

Prayer & meditation: Within the American religious community, prayer is the sanctioned route to communication with God. Whether group or individual, the essence of prayer *is* this connection— "…from our mouths to God's ear." Meditation, or personal, contemplative prayer, is also becoming more accepted in Judeo-Christian traditions. Both of these activities are important in the life of the faithful person seeking peace and comfort. Those of us with this goal may pray several times each day, and some even describe their days as "one constant prayer to God". Whether the prayer is continual or intermittent, it serves as a reminder of God's accessibility and constancy in our lives.

Music: Melody has the ability to touch souls like nothing else on earth. It seems that those individuals who are drawn to the element of Feelings are particularly susceptible to music's powers. Whether played, sung, or merely listened to, music is an almost essential part of spirituality for those of us drawn to Feelings. Sometimes the notes of a Beethoven concerto or violin solo will create feelings of spirituality, but music from weekly services is most often the trigger for a strong emotional connection to our faith.

The Path of Feelings in Example

The mystical side of faith is extremely appealing to those who choose the path of Feelings. Investigating and nurturing the mystical path to God and Godliness can create emotional connections with faith that are extremely enriching; William James, one of the early pioneers of psychology, used called mystical experiences one hallmark of true faith. In mysticism, we put aside our intellect and create a purely emotional or "numinous" experience, one that cannot adequately be explained with words. Many faithful people over the ages have reported episodes when they felt tremendously close to God; these happenings touch on the essence of mysticism.

Among those who exemplify the path of Feelings, the

Baal Shem Tov (Master of the Good Name), also called the Besht, is one strong example. This 18th century rabbi founded the <u>H</u>asidic movement in eastern Europe, a movement based upon prayer as the main pathway to God. Before his appearance, study and scholarship were seen as the only proper route to personal spirituality, and only possible for the learned. His emphasis on joy, humility and spontaneity gave the "common" Jew a path to God, and he encouraged all Jews to participate in meditative prayer which allowed them to reach *devekut*, a higher state of consciousness. The Besht's emphasis on emotional responses to faith is a hallmark of the aspect of Feelings.

Among current authors, Lawrence Kushner is a person likely to score highly on this aspect of faith. As an author he has written several modern classic works exploring Kabbalistic thought (Honey From the Rock; The River of Light: Spirituality, Judaism and Consciousness), the Hebrew Alphabet (The Book of Letters: A Mystical Hebrew Alphabet; The Book of Words: Talking Spiritual Life, Living Spiritual Talk), and other topics. As well as being great reading for those of us treading the path of Feelings, his word pictures speak to the essence of the path of Feelings:

> *Each lifetime is the pieces of a Jigsaw puzzle.*
> *For some there are more pieces.*
> *For others the puzzle is more difficult to assemble.*
> *Some seem to be born with a nearly completed puzzle.*
> *And so it goes.*
> *Souls going this way and that*
> *Trying to assemble the myriad parts.*[18]

Outside of the Jewish tradition, Thomas Merton is another illustration of one exploring mystical teachings and the path of Feelings. Raised in a family that emphasized aesthetics and beauty (his parents were both artists), he became a Trappist monk[19] at the age of 26. His writings described the links between Eastern mystical traditions and Christianity, including *Seeds of Contemplation*, *Life and Holiness*, and *Mystics and Zen Masters*. His works have encouraged many to explore the mystical side of Christianity, and he has become one of the most famous American Roman Catholics of this century.

Practices To Expand This Aspect

Most individuals following this path have found several ways to invoke feelings of love and comfort. Here are some suggestions to get you started:

1. *Create a home "meditation space" that is relaxing and peaceful.* Dedicate space to meditative practices, and you will create a commitment to do it. A meditation space can be as small as an unused corner of a bedroom or a 3-foot-square area in the garden.

2. *Commit to 15 minutes of meditation each day.* Jewish meditation does exist; there are several books on the subject. Consistent practice gets better results, and it serves as a reminder to include faith in each day's activities.

3. *Take regular walks along the beach, an open field, or by a natural stream.* The connection of God with nature is a strong one, and when you are surrounded by nature an automatic sense of being close to God follows closely.

4. *Begin a spiritual journal.* Journal-writing is a wonderful way to express your innermost thoughts, and it helps to describe the internal emotions that are difficult to express out loud. Write down the important phrases, incidents and thoughts during your day.

5. *Use a picture of a beautiful spot in nature as a focus for meditation or prayer.* God in nature becomes even more apparent when used as a focal point for spiritual thoughts.

6. *Set your watch alarm to remind you to pray each day.* A perfect way to bring God into everyday life is to say morning, afternoon, and evening prayers.

7. *Write a Jewish short story.* Often, Feeling individuals are good with words, and exploring what imaginary characters believe is an excellent way to determine your own beliefs.

8. *Before beginning ritual prayer (or after completing one), sit quietly and just "listen".* We are most open to the "still small voice" when we empty our mind of ongoing thoughts. Often this can be a time of clearest connection to God.

9. *Create a quiet spot with plants and natural objects in which to meditate or pray.* In today's urban lifestyle, nature may not be close by. We can create our own "nature space" with plants in pots, stones, and other objects that can serve as a place for meditation or prayer.

10. *Learn melodies for some important prayers.* The music has a subtle connection to the prayer and thus to God. When you hum the melody throughout the day you create a reminder of faith.

11. *Memorize some traditional prayers from the faith.* Judaism has common prayers and those that are used less often. When you learn a little-known prayer, you create a sense of involvement with your faith.

12. *Learn to sing or play Jewish songs or melodies.* The

emotional responses that music releases can be even stronger when the music come from within ourselves. If you have not played the flute or piano in years, pick it up and start playing again.

13. *Read religious poetry or fables.* Poetry and allegorical tales appeal to the emotions as opposed to the intellect, and can reveal a new way to express faith in those drawn to this path.

14. *Play tapes or CDs with religious music.* Use the positive emotional reaction to music as a natural way to enjoy a spiritual experience throughout the day. Play it in the car, during meals, or while you prepare for the day.

15. *Find a book of meditations and read from it daily.* Jewish and non-Jewish authors have given us great words that inspire our sense of faith. Use their works on a regular basis to open daily prayer or begin your day on a positive note.

Enriching The Journey

The internal rewards of faith are great, and it is tempting to remain focused on this particular aspect of faith. But mature faith requires that we combine all four expressions of spirituality. We have said before that a full house of worship has four walls, and we anchor our positive feelings to the solid walls formed by information, connections, and guidance. Combining Feelings with Friends, for example, allows us to reveal the rewarding nature of faith to those around us. Feelings and Focus together communicate the peace that comes from having a sure direction for life. And the impact of Feelings upon the path of Fact can show confidence that even though we don't know everything, faith is still possible.

14
Friends: The Search for Relationship

*Life is to be fortified by many friendships. To love
and be loved is the greatest happiness of existence. (Sydney Smith)*

ᘓ   ᘓ   ᘓ   ᘓ   ᘓ

Susan is a forty-ish small business owner with a warm
and inviting manner. She converted to Judaism at the age of
thirty-nine, saying "It just seemed like coming home—it was the
weirdest thing! I read a book on world religions, and the chapter
on Judaism fascinated me. I decided to learn more about it, and
everything I read kept pulling me in. After I attended High
Holidays services I was hooked. I hadn't planned on converting,
but after the holiday services it became something I couldn't
'not do'." Susan is involved in the operation of her temple,
Joining her friend Naomi on many committees. Although
complaining of the hours required, they both enjoy the
interactions with others who are equally involved with her place
of worship.

Most of Susan's close friends are Jewish ("Isn't that
strange!" she says. "I wasn't born Jewish, but yet I relate best to
other Jews!"), and she attends weekly services on a regular basis.

175

"The thing I like most about services," she adds, "is reciting the Sh'ma. I almost feel like the top of my head is lifted off and I can send my energy directly to God." The aspect of spirituality that Susan and Naomi relate to the most is the path of Friends: the desire to bind oneself to something larger, to become part of a unity that crosses boundaries of time and space.

Major Emphasis

For those whose current emphasis the aspect of Relationship, the statement "no one is an island" could not be truer. The spiritual focus of this Aspect involves creating connections with those around them, through social activities and shared experiences. They are attracted to the community aspect of Judaism, and create strong and lasting friendships in their synagogues or JCC. The goal of the Friends pathway is unity with all creatures and all worlds...the "ultimate" connection.

Adults pursuing this path have a natural inclination to join group activities in their congregations. They have discovered the joyous truth that faith works well when mixed with people; a "melting pot" of faith is an excellent way to learn more about one's own beliefs. Members of this group also enjoy sharing spirituality. Those people following this path do not particularly want to *discuss* faith, they simply want to *share* their enjoyment with others. Whenever they think of faith, it is always in connection with others.

According to many rabbis it's impossible to be Jewish by yourself. Most Jews, and particularly those using the aspect of Friends, define themselves as part of the Jewish culture. We can't imagine being Jewish without a community to surround us. Jewish communities are like families: even when you hate them, you love them. We have learned that the Jewish community will always be there, asking for our time, talent and *tzedakah*. Through the viewpoint of Friends we welcome its presence, knowing that only surrounded by the Jewish community can we truly experience what it is to be a Jew.

Internal & External Aspects

As with the other spiritual factors, the aspect of relationship (Friends) is comprised of two manifestations—an inward and an outward presentation . The *outward* element seeks connection with other individuals through social contacts; the *internal* element looks for connection across time or space.

Looking outward: For most of us following this path, the element of connection has a social flavor. Just as Susan has shifted her friendships to focus on those with similar religious beliefs, the main social group for Friends-focused individuals usually comes from their congregation. Synagogue fund-raisers, picnics, and coffee with friends after services become major social activities that are truly satisfying in a spiritual sense. These activities create bonds that authenticate the need to be "one among many". Participation in these activities confirm the feeling that "yes, I am in the right place. I am connected to these people." More than a need for social contact, this outward focus satisfies the need to feel part of a larger whole, to bond to others who share common beliefs and experiences.

Looking inward: Another way to become part of a larger whole is by connecting through time or space. Those with an inward "Friends" focus find value in connecting with the *tradition* of their faith. Taking comfort from knowing that millions of others are performing exactly the same acts at the same time, or thinking "this ritual has been performed for centuries—I'm doing what my ancestors did!" are examples of this internal sense of spirituality. Using age-old words to light

Shabbat candles invokes this feelings for many individuals.

Others who share an internal focus on Friends look for a connection not with people but with God. Susan's sense of being connected to God through the Sh'ma is one example. Another woman emphasized that "...the utmost benefit (of faith) is to build a relationship with God. As a parent, it is very important to have God as a guide and a friend and also in our relationship with one another ...it is very important as a center of our relationship."

Fundamental Truth Of Friends

For the path of Friends, we find the common thread woven throughout that *God is in all, of all, and through all.* For those who pursue this Aspect, the truth of universal unity is inescapable. The aspect of Friends offers the opportunity to truly experience the connection to each other and to God. To those who follow this path the universal unity becomes real and tangible, and its truth inescapable.

> *There can be no vulnerability without risk; there can be no community without vulnerability; there can be no peace, and ultimately no life, without community. (M. Scott Peck)*

      ଔ   ଔ   ଔ   ଔ   ଔ

Most Rewarding Activities

Religious social functions: Those of us exploring the aspect of relationship enjoy being with others in their faith. We often develop close friendships within our congregations as we fulfill our primary desire for companionship and connection. It is not merely being with people that is important, but rather the connection to "others like me" that is critical. Those of us with a spiritual side tend to think and talk certain ways, and it is more comfortable when these thoughts can be shared without explanations. Gatherings with others who share the same spirituality make us feel as though we are "home".

Practice of rituals: Religious ritual offers an immediate bond with others; we can connect across time when we utter the Sh'ma as it has been recited for centuries, or across space as we retell the Passover story on the same day as all other Jews in the world. When we attend Shabbat services on a regular basis we also experience this connection. As we look around our congregation and behold a sea of faces worshiping as one, we strengthen our feelings of connection and relationship.

God in nature: Still another way that this Aspect unfolds is in the experience of the world around us. Audra, a single mother, described a recent rip to Hawaii. "I walked into a bamboo forest, and the trees were so dense that it was almost black. I sat down for a minute to get my bearings, and noticed that the wind was rustling through the bamboo. It was like the bamboo whistles that you get—each one vibrating at its own frequency and creating a sort of mystical melody. I thought to myself—this is God's music!" Connecting to God through nature is a common experience—sitting by the seashore and being awed by the power of universal forces, walking through a forest and seeing the face of God in the trees, sifting through sand and remarking on the insignificance of each human life are each ways in which we acknowledge the presence of God in all things.

The Path Of Friends In Action

Throughout history individuals have demonstrated the aspects of Fact, Feeling, Friends and Focus even though they have not been described in those terms before this. An example of a religious thinker with great affinity for the path of Friends was Martin Buber, Jewish 20th-century philosopher. Throughout his life he encouraged building bridges (connections) between various groups, first between Jews and Palestinians and later with Jews and Christians. In his most famous work, "I and Thou", he described the relationship between self and others, and between self and God. To Buber, humans are not complete until they find their personal pathway to connect with God. An individual more totally focused on connection would be difficult to find.

We find a biblical example of this path in the Biblical book of Esther, whose story offers lessons about the value of community. The story of Esther, Mordecai and Haman shows us that God can sometimes not seem present, but still work in the world. Esther, a Jew, is purchased to be the wife of a great ruler who knows nothing of her background, only that she is beautiful. Shortly after she comes to live in the palace, Haman, the prime minister, suggests to the king that the Jews are making trouble and should be eradicated, to which the king agrees. Esther, safe in her palace, at first is unaware of the decree and does nothing. But her benefactor, Mordecai, reminds her of her upbringing, and little by little Esther begins to agree that something must be done to save *her* people. Although protected from death by her position and her secrecy with respect to her heritage, she decides to reveal herself to save her community. Risking her own death, she shows the ruler the consequences of genocide to the Jews. In the end, Haman himself is eliminated, Esther and Mordecai are exhalted, and the story becomes one to be celebrated each year at the festival of Purim. A sense of community runs deep in the Jewish people, and this biblical story is perhaps one of the first examples of the strength of that bond.

When we create ecumenical movements and interfalth councils we provide examples of the path of Friends at work building bridges between communities. American Jewish support for the state of Israel is another example of creating community regardless of geographic separation. At a more personal level, individuals who start congregational social groups also help to satisfy the desire for connection that this aspect embraces.

> *If somewhere in China today an individual were to work out for himself all the ethical and theological principles of Judaism, and live up to them, would that make him a Jew? My answer is no.... he would not be a Jew until he had associated himself with the fellowship, and had accepted the responsibilities and instruments of that fellowship. (Maurice Samuel)*

> ଔ   ଔ   ଔ   ଔ   ଔ

Practices to Expand this Aspect

There are many ways to follow the spiritual path of Friends. Here are fifteen possibilities, as described by individuals who are on this path:

1. *Attend a religious fund-raiser with friends.* Particularly for those with an outward emphasis, this activity meets social needs *and* allows the participant to give to a charitable cause he or she believes in.

2. *Visit a service at another congregation and participate fully.* When we are in an unfamiliar environment we can concentrate on the ritual elements of a service instead of our friends. Becoming involved in ritual creates a sense of "belonging" that crosses both time and space.

3. *Join a social group in the congregation.* Combining spiritual

and social needs is a common way of fulfilling this aspect. Many groups exist, from baking groups to study groups to parent groups; most individuals can find several groups of interest to them.

4. *Memorize some traditional prayers.* Judaism includes both common prayers and those that are used less often. Learning little-known prayers creates a sense of involvement with one's spirituality.

5. *Join a chat group or listserve.* An excellent way to expand relationships is through the virtual community. Interest groups on religion, and even on specific topics within Judaism, are quite common and easy to find.

6. *Stay after services and chat with friends.* Again, combining social and spiritual needs is rewarding on both levels.

7. *Begin attending services on a regular basis, and meet some new people.* Oftentimes we are unaware of the opportunities for friendships in our own congregation. Notice the similarities between others and ourselves creates a greater sense of connection.

8. *Set aside a certain time for prayer each day.* Preserve time to communicate with God, and you create a sense of relationship with God.

9. *Read up on religious history to discover the age-old rituals and traditions.* A connection across time is an important element of the outward element of relationship. Learning about the founders of the faith creates a bond across decades and centuries.

10. *Practice the Jewish prayer method of hitbodenut—*

spontaneous prayer. Spontaneous prayer where thoughts are simply poured out to God creates a sense of God's constant presence. Although traditionally taking place in nature, the idea of simply speaking to God what is on your mind can be transferred to other settings as well.

11. *Make a point to speak with spiritual leaders on points of faith.* Relationship with God sometimes begins by relating to rabbis, cantors or other knowledgeable people. These discussions can begin or extend personal spiritual growth.

12. *Become involved in the larger Jewish community.* Connections extend beyond your own congregation. Find out what causes are important nationally and internationally, and build bridges across geographical boundaries.

13. *Start a Havurah that meets socially on a regular basis.* Create your own "friendship group". Add a religious emphasis, and the group becomes even more meaningful.

14. *Observe how others practice their faith.* We often become locked into certain practices, allowing our spirituality to become stale. Notice the practices of others, and you invigorate your spiritual life by suggesting new ways to celebrate faith.

15. *Find the history behind a common ritual.* Create a stronger bond with those in other centuries and other lands by knowing the historical context for a practice or prayer.

Enriching the journey

Pursuing the aspect of relationship, Friends, is extremely rewarding. Those of us following this path truly understand the concept of *tikkun olam* (healing the world). When we understand the concept that "all is one", we understand the importance of repairing what has gone wrong in our world. What affects one affects all, and through the path of Friends we can take action in this important area. Strengthening bonds with others strengthens the Jewish community—an important goal in assuring the continuity of the Jewish faith.

Combining the path with others strengthens our ties to faith and creates a more mature approach to Judaism. When we combine Friends with Feelings, we learn we can share our emotional fulfillment with others. Friends and Fact together can create exponential growth of our religious understanding by joining our knowledge with that of others. Lastly, exploring the path of Focus allows us to support others in their search for correct actions and beliefs. As you continue through life there will be many opportunities to enrich your faith; with Friends as a beginning, faith is guaranteed to flourish.

> *The core method of Judaism is community. Ours is not a personal testament, but a collective and public commitment; what defines the Jews as Jews is community; not values, not ideology. (Leonard Fein)*

ᘉ   ᘉ   ᘉ   ᘉ   ᘉ

15
Focus on 'Focus'

*The important thing is not how many separate
commandments we obey, but the spirit in which
we obey them. (Israel Baal Shem Tov)*

CB CB CB CB CB

For many of us, role models played an essential role in
our early development. Perhaps an aunt, a favorite teacher, or our
parents served as a set of snapshots of how to live our life. This
is the essence of Focus—finding guidance for each decision we
make. Chuck, a retired salesman on the path of Focus, spoke
about the guidance he received during some difficult financial
times. He says that he just sensed "a thing" that repeated a
scriptural citation over and over. "I looked up what it said and it
was this whole reading about how much God loves us and just
look how he takes care of flowers and trees, and if he takes such
good care of them just think what He is going to do for you—all
you have to do is just believe. I go 'Wow, this is powerful!' and
that was just His way of communicating with me, to speak to
me."

 Chuck's satisfaction came from a conviction that he was
"doing OK"; things were going the way they should. Following
guidelines that have been passed down through the centuries
provides comfort for those following the path of Focus; they feel
content when they know they are on the right path. For those of us

tending towards the perspective of Focus, expectations are important. What am I *supposed* to teach my children? How *should* I respond when asked to donate to charity? These are important questions that require specific answers, and those answers are found in the traditions of Judaism.

Major Emphasis

Looking through the lens of Focus, each personal action or choice is measured against a standard of perfection—we expect to make the correct choice. There seem to be far more choices today than ever before, and very rarely are these choices black and white. When we choose whether to help in a carpool or volunteer for a committee, or decide which charity deserves our donation, there often is not a right or wrong choice. The good news about Judaism is that it has been providing guidance for decision-making for centuries, for as we have heard "there is nothing new beneath the sun" (Ecclesiastes 1:9).

For those of us walking the path of Focus, our first requirement is for guidance based on our faith. When faced with difficult choices we ask our rabbi, discuss the issue with others from the congregation, or mention them in prayer. One of the hallmarks of this path is the desire to find the proper way of acting or responding *before* we make a choice. Sometimes this requirement means that decisions come slowly, often frustrating those around us. But for Focus, the important issue is choosing the correct direction. Nothing else is as critical, and therefor all else must wait its turn.

Another important sources of daily guidance comes from role models. For others role models may be good, but for those following the path of Focus they are essential. Whether these models are from the past or the present, they play an important part in a life focused on Focus. After the right choice is made, role models show us how to carry out our decisions. Role models demonstrate how real people practice peace, *tzedakah*, or other important values.

For many of us, our first role model is from summer camp. It's almost as if being away from our families creates a need to find a "surrogate parent" to teach us how we should behave. We see a fellow camper acting as we know we *should* act, and it suddenly becomes clear to us that there *is* a way to practice our faith. We keep this individual's image in our mind and ask ourselves in tough situations "Now, what would so-and-so have done?"

Others have family members as their role models. They can tell long stories about their grandmother, father, or aunt and how they practice their faith. Often it takes some time to see the pattern: it's not until the teen years that we realize Mom or Aunt Ruth has been our model of Judaism for many years. The models we choose often last long well into adulthood; one Jewish homemaker always has her grandmother in mind when she thinks about a Jewish home. "I can still remember where she kept the Shabbat candlesticks", she says, "and she used to clean the house absolutely spotless for Shabbat. I try to do the same thing for my family."

Whether the role model is a family member, a friend, or a person from a book, the purpose is the same — to show us concretely how to enact the values of our faith. The message is a critical part of spirituality: we must turn our own ideals and beliefs into real-world activities rather than keep them locked away in our heads. Focus is where ideas become reality. Without guidance put into action, our faith becomes hollow.

Internal & External Aspects

The path of Focus is not as easily divided into internal and external emphases. The other three paths have rather cleanly separated components, and a person normally is attracted either to the internal or external component. With Focus the two orientations seem to be intertwined, and both orientations are normally found in the same individual.

Looking inward: The internal segment of Focus emphasizes understanding values and performing personal acts (attending services, prayer). This orientation emphasizes the internal values, those that originate with our behavior and then affect others. The inward emphasis also addresses how we react when faced with problem situations. We might, for example, use this aspect to decide how to react when we hear gossip about a neighbor or fellow congregant.

Looking outward: This orientation, although closely tied to the internal emphasis, is more focused on the actions that are enacted *towards* others. Working on social action projects, volunteering, performing mitzvot and other visible acts are the emphasis here. This is the part of faith that populates volunteer programs and funds important causes, creating the visible acts of *tzedakah* and *ḥesed* that prove faith has an impact on our world.

Fundamental Truth Of Focus

For those following the path of Focus, discovering the code of ethical behavior is their God-given mission. *God shows the way* is the watchword, and conforming to God's expectations is pursued with great persistence. Whether through searching scripture, reading commentary, or performing mitzvot, we are in a constant search for a higher, better self that can be found only in understanding the goals set for us by God.

Most Rewarding Activities

Practicing mitzvot: The 613 *mitzvot* that form the core of Judaism are God-given ways to fulfill the expectations of faith. We follow the path of Focus and its emphasis on proper and appropriate guidelines when we practice the commandments for saying blessings, eating the proper foods, and praying in prescribed ways at prescribed times. Adults who have this factor of faith as a primary orientation often emphasize these practices above all else, for the *mitzvot* give us a natural and obvious way in which to be spiritual. This large group of adults enjoys having ritual acts involved in all parts of their day; the rituals serve as a constant reminder of God's presence in all affairs.

Social projects and volunteering: Another important emphasis of this aspect involves increasing religion's impact on the world. While performing *mitzvot* is a way of acknowledging God *within* the religious community, participation in activities for the social good displays our commitment *outside* of the Jewish community, or to society at large. This involvement is not meant to call attention to ourselves as pious individuals, but rather to call attention to God and the impact of faith in the world. When we volunteer our time and talents to causes we believe in, we follow the examples set by our role models and demonstrate a commitment to *tikkum olam*, or repairing the world.

Rituals and ceremonies: Performing rituals in a defined manner is important to those of us seeking guidance or Focus. We know that the prescribed order of a Shabbat service did not just happen by accident; the sages and rabbis who created it had a particular purpose in mind. When we follow this order we again receive satisfaction that we are "doing as we should", and that God would want us to be exactly where we are. Lighting Shabbat candles in a particular way at a certain time, preparing for Passover in a prescribed manner, or praying certain prayers at certain times are all ways that we can participate in God's plan, knowing that wiser individuals than ourselves understood the reasons behind the plan. Sometimes it is not up to us to know the reasons, only to follow in the path that has been prepared for us.

The Path of Focus in Example

Many spiritual leaders have exemplified the path of Focus in their commitment to values, ritual, and mitzvot. This path can be seen in the life of Rabbi Moshe ben Maimon (Maimonides) and in the biblical history of the Judge Devorah.

Maimonides lived in Spain in the early 1100s, descended from a long line of rabbis. Trained as a physician, he is now known for his major commentary on the *Mishnah*, or Oral Torah, and his Book of the Commandments (*Sefer HaMitzvot*) in which he lists the 613 commandments found in Torah. Even today, his list of the thirteen fundamental principles of Judaism is recited by many Jews on a daily basis. Maimonides was singularly focused on the rituals and expectations of Judaism, creating the most extensive listing of its commandments (*mitzvot*) to date. His conviction of the importance of Focus is emulated today, especially among Orthodox Jews.

Deborah, along with other judges in the Hebrew Bible, led a life committed to the practice of Jewish values and law. Deborah was a prophet as well as a judge, having a special ability to interpret law with respect to God's intentions. She was respected widely for her wisdom, knowledge, and piety, and people came great distances to ask for her judgement on their disputes. Her example shows the importance of combining law with Jewish values, creating a strong foundation upon which to base life's decisions.

In contemporary life, we see examples of Focus daily. Religious organizations that undertake projects to help the less privileged, and congregations who speak out for a cause they believe in are practicing the path of Focus. This spiritual path stands for values and action; it is where religion deals with the rigors of life.

Practices to Expand this Aspect

Quite a few ways exist in which this path to faith can be enhanced. Here are fifteen ideas to begin your own thinking processes:

1. *Join a weekly study group.* Be with faithful others on a regular basis to help bring Judaism into life situations.

2. *Read about famous Jews and their lives.* Learn how Jews in the past led faithful lives, and you provide a way to bring faith into your own life.

3. *Increase the number of mitzvot you perform.* Most of us are a long way from performing all possible commandments in Torah. Add another *mitzvot* each month and grow in your practice of faith.

4. *Make a commitment to volunteer for a worthwhile cause.* When we practice our faith in the world, we expand the positive effects of our faith to touch others.

5. *Find new holiday rituals to enrich your faith.* Most holidays have special foods and traditions that add a sense of specialness to the day. Find new ways to celebrate and enrich your sense of faith.

6. *Create a self-study program for yourself.* A perfect way to learn more about the expectations of faith is to study on a regular basis. There are many commentaries to choose from—find one that you can use weekly.

7. *Hang a Jewish calendar where you can see it daily.* Simply knowing the Jewish date can bring a sense of Judaism to your

days and remind us of the yearly cycle of Jewish life.

8. *Find a new cause and begin making regular contributions.*
The Jewish tradition of tzedakah is enriched if you find a
particular cause you care about and follow its progress.

9. *Begin (or increase) daily prayers.* Judaism has structured
times for prayer; add afternoon or morning prayers to your day
and see how faith permeates your life.

10. *Head up a social action project in your congregation.* Show
your commitment to faith in action—care for the sick, provide
for the needy. These "random acts of kindness" are powerful
ways to enrich personal Judaism.

11.*Find out what rituals are being performed by others in your
congregation.* Friends and acquaintances can be an excellent
source of ideas to enrich your faith.

12. *Talk to people older than yourself about their practice of
Judaism.* Those with more experiences behind them can be
important role models and give us examples to follow.

13. *Watch movies with Jewish content.* There are many excellent
films out there that contain important Jewish themes and address
significant issues. Watch them to remind yourself of these
essential ideas.

14. *Get a complete list of the mitzvot and learn how to practice
them.* There are excellent sources with background of each
commandment; understanding is a step closer to doing.

15.*Read books about the experiences of Jews in other countries.*
Judaism is practiced differently is various places. You can

probably find a custom from another nation that speaks to you in a positive way.

Enriching The Journey

Some would say that Focus' emphasis on performing mitzvot is the core of Judaism. Following Jewish values and performing commandments is clearly following God's expectations for the Jewish people, and for many this is all that is required to be a "good Jew". Yet, without the other Aspects it creates a hollow faith: one that has no intellectual content or personal connection. It is true that there is not a standard set of beliefs to be uncovered by Fact or a "correct" emotion to be experienced through Feelings, but when we add the study of Torah, membership in the Jewish community, and a personal emotional connection to our Focus-related practices, we create a strong foundation in faith that will withstand the pushes and pulls of life.

ଔ   ଔ   ଔ   ଔ   ଔ

Epilogue

When you love Adonai Elohecha body and soul
These things I ask of you will be possible:
To answer your children's questions about Me
And believe your answers yourselves
To connect religion to your everyday
comings and goings...
for example,
When you hug them in bed at night
With tender words—Sh'ma Yisrael
Or when you think to say Modeh Ani
In the rush of getting them up and out
In the morning
To be alert enough
to open doors for your children
in every waking moment
and when they dream.
And finally, to remember just why
all these things matter:
They matter because I, Adonai Elohecha,
brought you and your children out of Egypt
to be God for you.
I am your God.
And when you do these things
I will be your children's God.

("V'AHAVTA:When You Love", by Rabbi Sheldon Marder)

ଔ   ଔ   ଔ   ଔ   ଔ

One early criticism of this book was made by a reviewer who said "I don't know if it's really possible to raise a spiritual child." The previous chapters give evidence that the task is certainly possible, and in fact *likely* if you are committed to the outcome..."when you do these things, I will be your children's God". Some rabbis believe that God instills in each of us the desire to connect in some meaningful way to God and the sacred. Life is a matter of realizing this desire and then finding ways to make a meaningful connection between ourselves and holiness. Kabbalists speak of the spark in each of us that yearns to be connected to other sparks and through them to God. If these ideas are true, every child will sooner or later create his own link to faith. It is our mission as parents, grandparents and concerned caregivers to assist them on this path, forging a link strong enough to withstand every challenge that life has to offer.

We have help with this task. The Jewish community stands ready to help in every way it can—through synagogue membership, Jewish cultural events, Jewish day schools and vacation camps. Our Jewish Community Centers and Bureaus of Jewish Education are valuable partners in guiding our children along the path to a strong Jewish commitment. The message here? Become involved in your Jewish community however you can. Find Jewish websites. Attend Jewish plays and concerts. Get on Jewish mailing lists and join Jewish book clubs. Find creative ways to bring Judaism into your children's daily lives. Children learn best from what is around them—make it impossible for them to *not* think Jewishly.

As Jews, we have a faith that can satisfy each of the four needs mentioned here: for understanding, for comfort, for connection, and for guidance. While many of us look to fulfill these desires in other faiths, like Dorothy in The Wizard of Oz we can find everything we need in our own back yard. There is a story from Rabbi Nachman of Bratslav about a poor rabbi who needs money to build a synagogue for his congregation. Every night he dreams of a bridge in Vienna under which is buried a bag of gold. After dreaming this dream for many nights he travels to Vienna and looks under the bridge. After searching and digging, he runs into a guard who asks what he's doing. When he hears the dream, the guard laughs and says "I, too, have a dream. I dream that a poor rabbi has gold under his stove!" The rabbi returns home, removes the floorboards from under his stove, and there finds the gold he needs.

We Jews are often like the poor rabbi. We become Buddhists to find Feelings, fundamental Christians for Focus, or agnostics because we lack Facts. Yet, Judaism has all the gold one could ever need. In our tradition of Torah study we search for understanding and emphasize the aspect of Fact. Kabbalah provides incredible richness for those looking for the comfort of Feelings. For those looking for connection in Friends there is the Jewish community and the Havurah movement. And those looking for Focus (guidance) have the tradition of Jewish ethics and 613 commandments to provide direction. Each of the riches we look for in other faiths can be found in Judaism; our cup of gold overflows. It is all there for the enrichment of ourselves and our children.

Children raised to value their Jewish roots have an advantage in life. While our increasingly multicultural world gives us hundreds of choices, Judaism provides a well-proven set of expectations and values. Today religion means more than just blind faith; Judaism stands grounded in a lengthy tradition of study and analysis. And even though life in the 21st century is full of stressors at each turn, Jews can find comfort in age-old traditions and prayers. Psychologist Abraham Maslow stresses the importance of belonging and community; there is always a Jewish community ready to welcome each Jew. Parents who introduce their children to Judaism create a solid foundation for their child to build upon, stone by stone, from the experiences of life.

Raising a spiritual child is a large task, but it can be accomplished. With the resources and ideas presented here, assistance from the Jewish community, and your own commitment to Judaism, success is almost assured. You bought this book because you want the best for your child, and that desire is your most important asset as you set out to grow a child's faith.

When you become the best that *you* can be, your children and grandchildren will naturally follow your lead. As you pursue your own path to God and yourself become a "spiritual parent", a spiritual child is the natural result. May God bless you richly as you follow this path and give you peace along the way.

CS   CS   CS   CS   CS

Notes

[1] Proverbs 22:6

[2] Victor Frankl, *The Will to Meaning*, 1968.

[3] Hample & Marshall, *Children's Letters to God*, 1988.

[4] Among these were a group of 65 research participants who were interviewed on their faith. These individuals, referred by their clergy, provide many of the anecdotes found in the rest of the book.

[5] Martin Buber, *Way of Response*, 1971.

[6] Maimonides (Moses ben Maimon) was a Jewish scholar and writer in the 12th century.

[7] David Kiersey & Marilyn Bates, *Please Understand Me*, 1978.

[8] Babylonian Talmud, Berakhot 4a.

[9] Psalms 116:1. *Tanakh: The Holy Scriptures*. Jewish Publication Society, 1988.

[10] Radziszewska, B. et al., Journal of Behavioral Medicine, Volume 19(3), June 1996.

[11] Herz, L. and Gullone, E., Journal of Cross-Cultural Psycohlogy, Volume 30(6), November 1999.

[12] Pruett, K., Families in Society, Volume 74(1), January 1993.

[13] A story is told in Leviticus Rabbah of the 100-year-old who was planting trees by the side of the road. When the emperor Hadrian saw the old man, he asked the man, "Do you expect to eat the fruit of the trees?" "If I am worthy, I will eat," said the old man. "But if not, as my father worked for me, I work for my children."

[14] Babylonian Talmud, Gittin 6b

[15] Babylonain Talmud, Yevamot 63a

[16] This emphasis on perpetual searching has also been called a "quest" approach by those studying faith, particularly Gregory Batson. The dimension of Quest has been described as emphasizing the search rather than the answers, similar to the Aspect of Intellect.

[17] Evelyn Underhill, *Mysticism*, p. 71.

[18] Lawrence Kushner, *Honey from the Rock*, 1990.

[19] The Catholic order of Cistercians (Trappists) is known for their observance of strict silence, participation in hard manual labor, and dietary restrictions.